PETITE

Presents

*beautiful knit projects
made with 150g or less*

BY KNIT PICKS

Photography by Amy Cave

Printed in the United States of America

Second Printing, 2016

ISBN 978-1-62767-105-7

Versa Press, Inc

800-447-7829

www.versapress.com

CONTENTS

KIMBERLEY COWL

by Laura Reinbach

FINISHED MEASUREMENTS

24" circumference x 8.5" high

YARN

Knit Picks Capretta (80% Fine Merino
Wool, 10% Cashmere, 10% Nylon; 230
yards/50g):

MC Sagebrush 26563, C1 Platinum 25595,
C2 Caviar 25593, 1 ball each

NEEDLES

US 4 (3.5mm) 24" circular needles, two
pairs plus a spare DPN or needle, or size
to obtain gauge

NOTIONS

Yarn Needle
Stitch Markers
Scrap Yarn
Crochet Hook

GAUGE

24 sts and 30 rows = 4" in stranded St st
in the round, blocked

Kimberley Cowl

Notes:

This reversible fair isle cowl is provisionally cast on and knit for 8.5", following a chart. Next, the colors are switched, and knit for another 8.5", following a second chart. The last half is folded into itself and the live stitches are grafted to the provisional cast on stitches via the three needle bind off. This creates a cozy, warm, double thick cowl.

When working the fair isle section, make sure you stretch out your stitches on the right hand needle before changing colors. This helps keeps your floats nice and loose and prevents your knitting from puckering.

Crocheted Provisional Cast On

http://tutorials.knitpicks.com/wptutorials/crocheted-provisional-cast-on/

3-Needle Bind Off

* Hold the two pieces of knitting together with the points facing to the right. Insert a third needle into the first st on each of the needles K-wise, starting with the front needle. Work a knit st, pulling the loop through both of the sts you've inserted the third needle through. After pulling the loop through, slip the first st off of each of the needles. Repeat from *. Pass the first finished st over the second and off of the needle.

See also the tutorial at: http://tutorials.knitpicks.com/wptutorials/3-needle-bind-off/

DIRECTIONS

With scrap yarn, provisionally CO 144 sts.

Row 1: With MC, K across.

Next Row: PM and join in round, begin Chart 1.

Work rows 1-39 of Chart 1 once, then work rows 1-26 for a total of 65 rounds, reading each row from right to left. Repeat the chart 6 times across the round. Piece should measure approximately 8.5" from CO.

With C2:

K 1 rnd.

P 1 rnd.

K 1 rnd.

Next, start Chart 2. Work rows 1-39 of Chart 2 once, then work rows 1-26 for a total of 65 rounds, reading each row from right to left. Repeat the chart 6 times across the round. Do not BO.

Finishing

Weave in ends.

Either leave live sts on needle or place on scrap yarn for blocking. Cut C1 and C2 yarn. Leave MC ball attached to use for 3-Needle Bind Off. Block.

Transfer scrap yarn sts back to circular needle, if needed. Place provisional CO sts onto extra circular needle. Fold half of cowl into itself with wrong sides facing. The purl row creates one end and both pairs of needles should be next to each other at the other end. Arrange sts on the two needles so they line up exactly with each other. Graft your live sts together using the 3-Needle Bind Off method. Weave in last end.

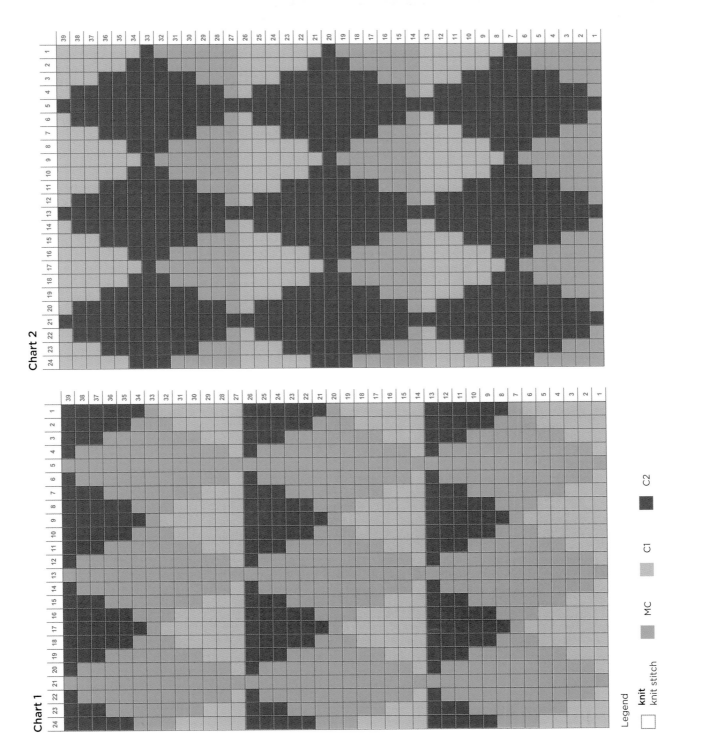

Chart 2

Chart 1

Legend

knit

knit stitch

MC

C1

C2

BLACK AND WHITE CLUTCH

by Faye Kennington

FINISHED MEASUREMENTS

8" wide x 5" high x 1" deep

YARN

Knit Picks Gloss DK (70% Merino Wool, 30% Silk; 123 yards/50g): MC Cream 24985, C1 Black 24722, C2 Tranquil 26077, 1 ball each.

NEEDLES

US 6 (4mm) 16" circular needles, or size to obtain gauge

US 4 (3.5mm) 16" circular needles, or two sizes smaller than needles used to obtain gauge

NOTIONS

Yarn Needle

Stitch Marker

Thread to match C2

Sewing Needle

8" or longer Zipper

GAUGE

24 sts and 26 rows = 4" in stranded St st in the round on larger needles, blocked.

Black & White Clutch

Notes:

This bag is knit in one piece as a tube, with a bottom flap and top flaps that are sewn into place.

Using a larger needle size for the stranded section helps keep gauge consistent throughout the stitch pattern changes.

When working flat, follow the chart on RS rows from right to left, and WS rows from left to right. To work in the round, all chart rows are followed from right to left, as RS rows.

DIRECTIONS
Bottom Flap

With MC and larger needles, CO 50 sts using backwards loop cast on. Begin working flat.

Row 1 (RS): MC K1, *work Chart A Row 1; rep from * to last st, MC K1.

Row 2 (WS): Sl1, *work Chart A Row 2; rep from * to last st, WYIB Sl1.

Work next 4 rows of Chart A as established, maintaining selvedge st on edge.

Sides

Setup Rnd: MC K1, *work Chart B Rnd 1; rep from * to last st, MC K1, using MC CO 58 sts. 108 sts.

Join in rnd being careful not to twist. Sl 1st st to left hand needle, PM. Cut C1 and rejoin at start of rnd.

Work from Chart B through Rnd 10, then work Rnds 1-10 once more.

Work Rnds 1-4 of Chart C twice, repeating the chart row 27 times across the rnd.

Switch to smaller needles and MC, K 3 rnds.

Border

Switch to C2.

Rnd 1: K to end.
Rnd 2: P to end.
Rnds 3 & 5: (K1, P1) to end.
Rnd 4: (P1, K1) to end.

Zipper Flaps

Setup Rnd: (P48, BO next 6 sts) twice. Work the remaining 2 groups of 48 sts separately, flat.

Row 1: K48.
Row 2: K48.

BO all 48 sts.

Cut yarn and work above 2 rows on remaining 48 sts, BO.

Finishing

Weave in ends.

Fold and sew the bottom flap edges (A & C) to the cast on edge of the tube (B & D). Catch the cast on and selvedge edges into the seam for the neatest appearance.

Sew the short edges of the zipper flaps (E) to the 6-st BO edges of the bag sides at the top (H).

Using the thread and sewing needle, sew the zipper into the slit at the top of the bag (G). You can evenly whip stitch through each BO st into the zipper for a clean look. If the zipper is longer than the bag, you can tuck the closed end into the bag. Do not stretch the knitted work as you sew in the zipper or the bag will be distorted.

Wash and block to finished measurements. If using an iron, take note of appropriate settings for silk.

Chart A

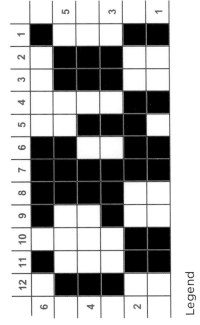

Legend

knit
☐ RS: knit stitch
WS: purl stitch

☐ MC
■ C1

Chart B

Chart C

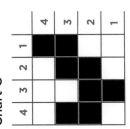

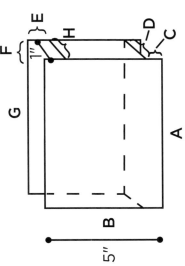

5"

CHEERY AMELIA HAT

by Danna Rachel Cauthern

FINISHED MEASUREMENTS

16, (17.75, 19.5)" circumference

YARN

Knit Picks Wool of the Andes (100% Peruvian Highland Wool, 110 yards/50g):

Color Block Version: MC Blossom Heather 25067, C1 White 24065, C2 Tranquil 25981, 1 ball each. Solid Version: Dove Heather 24077, 1 (1, 2) balls.

NEEDLES

US 8 (5mm) 16" or 24" circular needle, plus preferred method for working in the round, or size needed to obtain gauge

NOTIONS

Size H (5 mm) crochet hook

Stitch Markers

Scrap Yarn or Stitch Holder

Yarn Needle

2.5" Pom-Pom Maker (optional)

GAUGE

18 sts and 28 rows = 4" in K1, P3 Rib Pattern in the round, blocked

Cheery Amelia Hat

Notes:

Cheery Amelia is a seamless earflap hat in 3 sizes, to fit anyone big or small. It is colorful without requiring complex colorwork. Different color and pom-pom options make Cheery Amelia versatile and fun. Its ribbed texture makes the hat stretchy for a cute, snug fit. It is a perfect stashbuster, using just around 50 grams!

The hat is knit from the bottom up, with the earflaps worked first. The earflaps are worked back and forth, and the hat body is worked in the round.

For neater color changes between color blocks worked in K1, P3 Rib Pattern, K all sts in the first round in the new color. Resume K1, P3 Rib Pattern in the second round.

To minimize "jogs" at the color change, work color changes as follows: With the new color, K one rnd. Before knitting the first stitch of the second round in the new color, pick up the stitch below that stitch (it will be in the old color) and place it on the needle without twisting. K or P the picked-up stitch together with the first stitch of the round.

Make 1 Left (M1L)

Insert left needle from front to back through strand in between sts and K this loop through back loop.

Make 1 Right (M1R)

Insert left needle from back to front through strand in between sts and K this loop.

Single Crochet

Begin with a slip knot on the hook. Insert hook from front to back through edge st. Bring yarn over hook to make a loop and pull the new loop through the edge st. Two loops remain. Bring yarn over hook and pull the new loop through both loops on the hook. One single crochet st made.

Slip Stitch – Crochet

With one st on the hook, insert hook from front to back through crochet st. Bring yarn over hook to make a loop and pull the new loop through the crochet st and the st on the hook. One crochet slip st made.

DIRECTIONS

Earflaps (all versions)

In C1, CO 5 (7, 7) sts using a long-tail cast-on.

Row 1 (WS): P1, K1 (2, 2), P1, K1 (2, 2), P1.
Row 2 (RS): K1, M1R, P1 (2, 2), K1, P1 (2, 2), M1L, K1.
Row 3 (WS): P1, K2 (3, 3), P1, K2 (3, 3), P1.
Row 4 (RS): K1, M1R, P2 (3, 3), K1, P2 (3, 3), M1L, K1, 9 (11, 11) sts.

Continue working earflap increases as established, working in K1,

P3 Rib and working the first and last st of each row in St st (K on RS, P on WS), and on each RS row working M1R after first st and M1L before last st until there are 19 (23, 23) sts. Incorporate the increased sts into the ribbing pattern as you go. End on a WS row. Cut yarn. Do not bind off.

Place first earflap on a piece of scrap yarn or stitch holder. With C1, work second earflap, ending on a WS row. Do not bind off or cut yarn.

Hat Body

With C1, work 19 (23, 23) earflap sts in K3, P1 Rib Pattern (including the first and last "edge" stitches previously worked in St st). CO 13 (13, 17) sts using backward loop cast-on.

Work 19 (23, 23) earflap sts in K3, P1 Rib Pattern (including the first and last "edge" stitches previously worked in St st). CO 13 (13, 17) sts using backward loop cast-on.

CO 21 (21, 25) sts using backward loop cast-on. Join to work in the rnd and PM to mark beginning of the rnd. 72 (80, 88) sts.

Work 1 rnd, maintaining the K1, P3 Rib Pattern on the earflap and establishing the ribbing pattern on the cast on stitches.

Color Block Version

Work in K1, P3 Rib Pattern until piece measures 1.25 (1.5, 1.5)" from CO edge of hat body. Change to MC. K one rnd. Work in K1, P3 Rib Pattern until MC block is 2.75 (3, 3)" and piece measures 4 (4.5, 4.5)" from CO edge of hat body, or when hat is about 2.5 (3.5, 3.5)" shorter than desired length from CO edge of hat body. Change to C2. K one rnd. Work in K1, P3 Rib Pattern until C2 block is 0.5 (1, 1)" and piece measures 4.5 (5.5, 5.5)" from CO edge of hat body.

One-Color Version

Work in K1, P3 Rib Pattern until piece measures 4.5 (5.5, 5.5)" from CO edge of hat body, or when hat is about 2 (2.5, 2.5)" shorter than desired length from CO edge of hat body.

Decreases

16" Size Only: Remove marker, P1, K1. Replace marker.

All Sizes:

Rnd 1: *P3, K1, P2, K2tog, PM, repeat from * to end of rnd. 9 (10, 11) sts dec. 63 (70, 77) sts.
Rnd 2: *P3, K1, P2, K1, repeat from * to end of rnd. (P all purl sts and K all knit sts to end of rnd).
Rnd 3: *P3, K1, P2, K1, P3 Rib Pattern until 2 sts before marker, k2tog, repeat from * to end of round. 9 (10, 11) sts dec.
Rnd 4: P all purl sts and K all knit sts to end of rnd.

Repeat Rnds 3 and 4 until 18 (20, 22) sts remain, switching to magic loop or DPNs when necessary. *K2tog, repeat from * to end of rnd, removing markers. 9 (10, 11) sts remain. Cut yarn. With yarn needle, pull end through remaining sts. Secure end.

Finishing

With MC, single crochet evenly around hat edge. Slip stitch into first single crochet, cut yarn, and pull yarn through to secure.

(Optional) With MC, make a 2.5" pom-pom. Secure to top of hat. Weave in ends. Block if desired.

COLORWORK CONVERTIBLE MITTENS

by Andrea Sanchez

FINISHED MEASUREMENTS

7 (8)" hand circumference x 8.5 (9.5)" length

YARN

Knit Picks Capretta (80% Fine Merino Wool, 10% Cashmere, 10% Nylon; 230 yards/50g):

MC Cream 25600, C1 Turmeric 25948, 1 ball each

NEEDLES

US 3 (3.25mm) straight or circular needles, plus DPN's or preferred method for working in the round, or size to obtain gauge

US 4 (3.5mm) straight or circular needles, or 1 size larger than gauge needle

NOTIONS

Yarn Needle

Stitch Markers

Scrap yarn or stitch holder

2 - 13mm buttons

Matching thread and Sewing needle

1" Pompom maker (optional)

GAUGE

28 sts and 38 rows = 4" in St st on smaller needles, blocked.

Colorwork Convertible Mittens

Mittens

Notes:

The hand of this mitt is knit flat, then seamed. Stitches are picked up below the top cuff and the top of the mitten is knit in the round.

On RS rows (odd numbers) the charts are followed from right to left, on WS rows (even numbers) the charts are followed from left to right.

I-cord

With dpn or short circular needle, CO 2 sts on a WS row. Work in established ribbing for 1.5" ending on a WS row.

Next Row: P2, *K2, P2, rep from * to end of row.

Work slide sts to right end of needle. CO 2 sts then without turning work slide sts to right end of needle. *K2 sts, without turning work slide sts to right end of needle. Repeat from * until i-cord measures desired length.

DIRECTIONS
Right Hand

With smaller needle and MC, CO 42 (50) sts.

Next Row: P2, *K2, P2, rep from * to end of row.

Work in established ribbing for 1.5" ending on a WS row.

Next Row (RS): K2 *M1, K5 (6), rep from * to end, 50 (58) sts.

Next Row (WS): P24 (28), PM, P2, PM, P to end.

Increase Row: Join C1 and begin working Right Mitten chart over next 24 (28) sts, then continue with MC; SM, M1R, K to next M, M1L, SM, K to end, 2 thumb gusset sts inc.

Next Row (WS): Purl.

Rep last 2 rows 9 times more. 70 (78) sts; 22 thumb sts.

Work as established for 2 rows, without any increases.

Next Row: Continue working Chart over first 24 (28) sts, remove M, place next 22 sts on waste yarn, backward loop CO 2 sts, K to end, 50 (58) sts.

Continue working as established until hand measures 5 (5.5)" from cuff CO or approximately 1" less than desired Mitten length without the Top, break C1 yarn.

Top Ribbing

Next Row: With MC, K2, *P2, K2, rep from * to end.

Work in established ribbing for 1".

BO all sts in ribbing loosely using larger needle.

Block mitt.

Use mattress stitch to seam side of hand from bottom cuff to top cuff.

Use darning needle and waste yarn to thread a lifeline through 24 (28) sts in the row directly before top ribbing on back of mitt (colorwork side).

Left Hand

Repeat Right Hand directions, until Increase Row.

Increase Row: With MC, K to M, SM, M1R, K to next M, M1L, SM, join C1 and begin working Left Mitten chart over next 24 (28) sts, 2 thumb gusset sts inc.

Next Row (WS): Purl.

Rep last 2 rows 9 times more, 70 (78) sts; 22 thumb sts.

Work as established for 2 rows, without any increases.

Next Row: Removing markers as you come to them, K to M, place next 22 sts on waste yarn, backward loop CO 2 sts, continue working Chart over final 24 (28) sts, 50 (58) sts.

Continue working as established until hand measures 5 (5.5)" from cuff or approximately 1" less than desired length, break C1 yarn.

Repeat Right Hand directions, from Top Ribbing to end.

Mitten top

With smaller needle and MC, CO 24 (28) sts.

Pick up 24 (28) sts from lifeline in MC, remove lifeline, PM, join to work in the rnd. 48 (56) sts.

Next Rnd: K1, *P2, K2; rep from * to last 3 sts, P2, K1.

Work ribbing as established for 5 rnds more.

Knit 2 rnds.

Join C1 and K 4 rnds.

Continue working in St st (K all sts) alternating 4 rnds of C1 with 4 rnds of MC until mitten top measures 2.5 (3)" from CO edge or 1" less than desired length.

Set-up Rnd: Maintaining stripe pattern, *K6 (8), PM; rep from * to end.

Decrease Rnd: Maintaining stripe pattern, *K to 2 sts from M, K2tog; rep from * to end of rnd. 8 (7) sts dec.

Rep decrease rnd every other rnd another 4 (6) times, until 8 (7) sts remain.

Next Rnd: *K2tog; rep from * to last 0 (1) st, K (0) 1, 4 sts.

Next Rnd: K2tog 2 times. 2 sts.

I-cord Button Loops

With MC and smaller needles work i-cord for 1", break yarn leaving tail to attach to mitt.

Thread tail of yarn through live sts, pull tight to fasten off.

Use darning needle to stitch i-cord to top of mitt to make a loop.

Repeat mitten top for second mitt.

Thumb

Place 22 thumb sts on smaller needles, using MC, PU 1 st from center CO, K22, PU 1 st from center CO, PM, join to work in the rnd. 24 sts.

Decrease Rnd 1: K1, K2tog, K to last 3 sts, SSK, K1. 2 sts dec.

Rnds 2-3: Knit.

Rep Rnds 1-3, two times more. 18 sts.

Work even in St st until thumb measures 1.75 (2)" separation from hand.

Decrease Rnd: *K4, K2tog; rep from * to end. 3 sts dec.

Rep Decrease Rnd every other rnd 3 times more. 6 sts.

Break yarn and pull through remaining sts.

Repeat for second thumb.

Finishing

Sew button to center back of wrist (colorwork side) of each mitten.

Use 1" pompom maker and C1 to make two pompoms. Sew pompom directly next to button.

Weave in ends, and block once more if desired.

Left Mitten Chart

Right Mitten Chart

Legend

knit
RS: knit stitch
WS: purl stitch

MC

CC

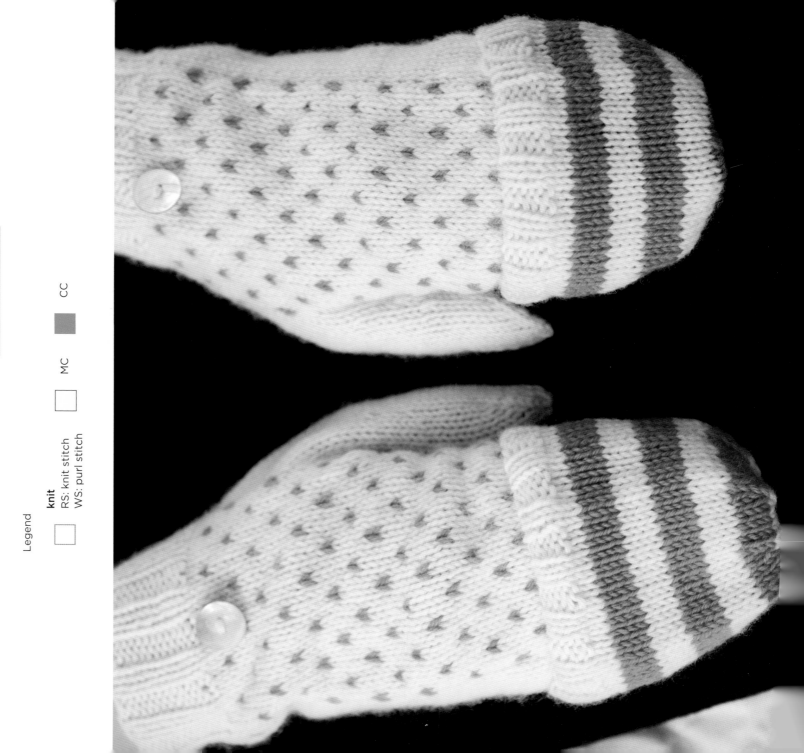

MINI KITTY POUF

by Molly Rivera

FINISHED MEASUREMENTS

12" high x 23" around

Yarn

Knit Picks Big Cozy (55% Superfine Alpaca, 45% Peruvian Highland Wool; 44 yards/100g): **Body, V1:** MC Hare Heather 26490, 2 balls; C1 Finnley Heather 26488, 1 ball. **Body, V2:** MC: Finnley Heather 26488, 2 balls; CC Cobblestone Heather 26484, 1 ball.

Knit Picks Tuff Puff Super Bulky (100% Wool, 44 yards/100g): **Face:** C2 Black 26837, 1 ball; **Nose:** C3 Pucker 26840, 1 ball

NEEDLES

US 15 (10mm) 16" circular needles, or size to obtain gauge

NOTIONS

Yarn Needle

Stitch Marker

Quilt Batting

Polyester Stuffing

GAUGE

8 sts and 12 rows = 4" in St st in the round, blocked.

Mini Kitty Pouf

Notes:

This is a simple pattern knit in Stockinette st in the round. The ears are worked by sewing the top corners together.

Stockinette stitch (St st, worked in the round over any number of sts)

All Rounds: Knit.

DIRECTIONS

CO 46 sts in MC, PM and join to work in the round, being careful not to twist sts.

Work 8 rounds in St st.

*Switch to C1, work 3 rounds in St st. Switch to MC, work 3 rounds in St st. Repeat from * 2 more times.

With C1 work 10 rounds in St st.

With MC work 8 rounds in St st.

BO all sts.

Finishing

The face is embroidered on the largest area of one color, the 10 rounds knit in C1. With C2 embroider face of kitty as shown with the stripes below it as the body. Use C3 as an option for a pink nose. Ears will be made on the ends above the face.

Ears

Sew together 5 sts at each end of the top of the kitty with MC to form the ears, leaving center sts unsewn. Thread a yarn needle with MC, cinch remaining sts together by picking up every 10th st on one side and then the other making a circle, pull the yarn tight and make a knot.

Weave in ends. Stuff the kitty by first lining it with quilt batting and then filling it with polyester stuffing.

Cinch the bottom sts shut in the same manner, using MC. Weave in any remaining ends.

Face Diagram

PINEY RIDGE NECKLACE

by Jeanie D. Maxey

FINISHED MEASUREMENTS

24" long, excluding toggle clasp

YARN

Knit Picks Galileo (50% Merino, 50% Viscose from Bamboo; 131 yards/50g):

Solid Necklace: C1 Gem, 26104 1 ball

Two Color Necklace: C1 Pearl, 26103; C2 White, 26094; 1 ball each

NEEDLES

US 4 (3.5mm) DPNs, or size to obtain gauge

NOTIONS

Yarn Needle
Stitch Holders
Jewelry Toggle Clasp Set

GAUGE

Left and Right Sections, Double-stranded rows: 7 rows = 1"

Middle Section, Single-stranded rows: 8 rows = 1"

(Gauge for this project is approximate, number of sts per inch does not matter.)

Piney Ridge Necklace

Notes:

The Left Section of this necklace is knitted to 9" long using two strands of yarn to make the I-cord. The Middle Section is "split" into two separate I-cords by placing every other stitch onto a stitch holder, while remaining stitches are kept on the DPNs and worked in I-cord to a length of 17". Then the working stitches are moved onto a new stitch holder while the remaining stitches that were previously placed on a stitch holder are worked in I-cord to a length of 17". The stitches of both I-Cords are then reunited by moving the stitches (alternating stitches) back onto the DPNs and the remaining 9" of the necklace is worked in I-cord with the two strands of yarn. After the necklace is completed, the Middle Section is twisted into a "Double Coin Knot". (See Double Coin Knot Photo Instructions.)

I-Cord

All Rows: K all sts in the row, then slide all sts from left side of needle to right side of needle, pulling yarn firmly behind work to form a tube.

DIRECTIONS

Left Section

While holding two strands of C1 together (or one strand each of C2 and C3 for two-color necklace), CO 5 sts. (You will have two sts in each of the 5 sets of sts across.) Slide all sts to right end of DPN. K all sts across. Cont in I-cord pat until Left Section measures 9" from beginning.

Middle Section, Separating I-Cord

While holding a stitch holder and a DPN in one hand, alternate loading one st onto stitch holder and one st onto DPN (or all C2 sts onto DPN and all C3 sts onto stitch holder for two-color necklace). You should have five 5 sts on stitch holder and 5 sts on DPN. Ignore sts on stitch holder for now. K all sts on DPNs in I-cord pat until Middle Section measures 17" from beginning. Move all these sts onto a new stitch holder. Using DPNs, pick up sts from 1st stitch holder and K all sts in I-cord pat until both pieces of Middle Section measure 17" from beginning of Middle Section.

Right Section

Being careful not to twist I-cords, alternate loading one st from stitch holder then one st from DPN onto new DPN until all sts are loaded onto the new DPN. K across row, combining both strands into each st, making up the original 5 sets of sts. Cont to K in I-cord pat until Right Section measures 9" from beginning of Right Section. BO all sts. Pull yarn through last st loop and lightly tug to tighten.

Creating Double Coin Knot

Step 1: Lay necklace on a hard, flat surface.

Step 2: Bring right end of I-cord up and over left end to form a loop, keeping the loop close to the I-cord junction of the necklace's Middle Section.

Step 3: Form a second loop and bring end of I-cord down to the right. (It should resemble a pretzel. Don't worry if one strand of the double I-cord loop appears slightly longer than the other, all will turn out well as the knot is completed.)

Step 4: Bend right end of I-cord under left I-cord end. (This end will be woven over the top left outside edge, under middle left intersecting loop, over middle right intersecting loop, and under the top right outside edge of the "coin knot" in the next step.)

Step 5: As noted in Step 4, the left I-cord is passed over the top left outside edge, under middle left intersecting loop, over middle right intersecting loop, and under the top right outside edge of the "coin knot".

Step 6: Gently pull the ends of the I-cord and manipulate the knot into shape.

Step 7: Your Double Coin Knot should look like this. If it doesn't, gently undo the knot and try again until you're happy with the final look.

Finishing

Using yarn needle and tail end of yarns on each end of necklace, securely sew each piece of toggle clasp onto appropriate end of necklace. Weave in and trim any excess yarn. Block before wearing.

ROOTED CABLE HAT

by Erica Jackofsky

FINISHED MEASUREMENTS

15.5 (18, 20.5)" relaxed finished circumference, 7 (7.5, 7.5)" length

YARN

Knit Picks Swish DK (100% Superwash Merino Wool; 123 yards/50g): Squirrel Heather 24948, 1 (2, 2) balls.

NEEDLES

US 5 (3.75mm) DPN's or preferred needles for working in the round, or size to obtain gauge

NOTIONS

Stitch Markers
Cable Needle

GAUGE

28 sts and 30 rows = 4" over 2x1 Ribbing in the round, relaxed.

For pattern support, contact Erica@FiddleKnits.com

Rooted Cable Hat

Notes:

Stitch markers shift 2 sts to the left on Rnd 33.

Chart is the same for all sizes. Only the number of times it is repeated will change. For the smallest size work the chart 7 times around. Medium repeats the chart 7 times. And the largest size will repeat the chart 8 times each round.

The crown decrease section is 18 rounds long (approximately 2.5"). As written, the hat will be 7 (7.5, 7.5)" from top of crown around. You can easily adjust the length by working more or less of the 2x1 Ribbing at the beginning, or add a bit of length by working some extra rounds even after rnd 26.

2x1 Ribbing (in the round over a multiple of 3 sts)
All Rnds: *K1, P1, K1; rep from * around.

Clx2 Right Purl
Sl 2 sts to CN and hold in back. K1, P2 from CN.

Clx2 Left Purl
Sl 1 st to CN and hold in front. P2, K1 from CN.

C2 over 2 Left
Sl 2 to CN and hold in front. K2, K2 from CN.

C3 over 3 Left
Sl 3 sts to CN and hold in front. K3, K3 from CN.

LT (Left Twist)
K into the back loop of the second st on the left needle then K into the front of the first st on the left needle. Let both sts drop from left needle. Alternately, transfer 1 st to CN and hold in front. K1, K1 from CN.

RT (Right Twist)
K into the second st on the left needle then K into the first st. Drop both sts from the left needle. Alternately, transfer one st to CN and hold back. K1, K1 from CN.

RTP (Right Twist Purl)
Sl one st to CN and hold back. K one st, P st from CN.

LTP (Left Twist Purl)
Sl 1 st to CN and hold in front. P1, K st from CN.

M1 (Make One)
PU the bar running between the st on your left and right needle. Place it on your left needle front to back. K it TBL. 1 st inc.

DIRECTIONS

Hat

CO 108 (126, 144) sts. PM and join to work in the rnd, being careful not to twist sts.

Work in 2x1 Ribbing for 1 (1.5", 1.5") or desired length of ribbing from CO.

Work Chart, or follow line-by-line directions, below.

Rnd 1 (RS): *K1, M1, (P1, RTP) twice, P1, LT, (P1, LTP) twice, P1, M1, K1; rep from * another 5 (6, 7) times.

Rnd 2: *(K1, P2) 3 times, K2, (P2, K1) 3 times; rep from * another 5 (6, 7) times.

Rnd 3: *K1 (P1, RTP) twice, P1, RT, LT, (P1, LTP) twice, P1, K1; rep from * another 5 (6, 7) times.

Rnd 4: *K1, P1, (K1, P2) twice, K4, (P2, K1) twice, P1, K1; rep from * another 5 (6, 7) times.

Rnd 5: *K1, RTP, (P1, RTP) twice, K2, (LTP, P1) twice, LTP, K1; rep from * another 5 (6, 7) times.

Rnd 6: *K2, P2, K1, P2, K1, P1, K2, P1, (K1, P2) twice, K2; rep from * another 5 (6, 7) times.

Rnd 7: *RTP, (P1, RTP) twice, P1, LT, (P1, LTP) three times; rep from * another 5 (6, 7) times.

Rnd 8: *(K1, P2) three times, K2, (P2, K1) 3 times; rep from * another 5 (6, 7) times.

Rnd 9: *(K1, RTP) twice, P1, RT, LT, (P1, LTP) twice, P1, K1; rep from * another 5 (6, 7) times.

Rnd 10: *K1, P1, (K1, P2) twice, K4, (P2, K1) twice, P1, K1; rep from * another 5 (6, 7) times.

Rnd 11: *K1, RTP, (P1, RTP) twice, K2, (LTP, P1) twice, LTP, K1; rep from * another 5 (6, 7) times.

Rnd 12: *K2, P2, K1, P2, K1, (K1, P2) twice, K2; rep from * another 5 (6, 7) times.

Rnd 13: *RTP, (P1, RTP) twice, P1, LT, (P1, LTP) three times; rep from * another 5 (6, 7) times.

Rnd 14: *(K1, P2) three times, K2, (P2, K1) 3 times; rep from * another 5 (6, 7) times.

Rnd 15: *K1, (P1, RTP) twice, P1, RT, LT, (P1, LTP) twice, P1, K1; rep from * another 5 (6, 7) times.

Rnd 16: *K1, P1, (K1, P2) twice, K4, (P2, K1) twice, P1, K1; rep from * another 5 (6, 7) times.

Rnd 17: *C1 over 2 Right Purl, (P1, RTP) twice, K2, (LTP, P1) twice, C1 over 2 Left Purl; rep from * another 5 (6, 7) times.

Rnd 18: *K1, P3, K1, P2, K1, P1, K2, P1, K1, P2, K1, P3, K1; rep from * another 5 (6, 7) times.

Rnd 19: *K1, P2, RTP, P1, RT, P1, LT, P1, LTP, P2, K1; rep from * another 5 (6, 7) times.

Rnd 20: *(K1, P2) twice, K2, (P1, K2) twice, (P2, K1) twice, rep from * another 5 (6, 7) times.

Rnd 21: *K1, C1 over 2 Right Purl, P1, RTP, LTP, K2, RTP, LTP, P1, C1 over 2 Left Purl, K1; rep from * another 5 (6, 7) times.

Rnd 22: *K2, P3, K1, P2, K4, P2, K1, P3, K2; rep from * another 5 (6, 7) times.

Rnd 23: *K2, P2, RT, P2, LT, P2, K2; rep from * another 5 (6, 7) times.

Rnd 24: *(K2, P2) twice, K4, (P2, K2) twice; rep from * another 5 (6, 7) times.

Rnd 25: *K2, C1 over 2 Right Purl, C1 over 2 Left Purl, K4, c1 over 2 right P, c1 over 2 left P, K2; rep from * another 5 (6, 7) times.

Rnd 26: *K3, P4, K6, P4, K3; rep from * another 5 (6, 7) times.

Rnd 27: *K1, K2tog, P4, K6, P4, SSK, K1; rep from * another 5 (6, 7) times. 108 (126, 144) sts

Rnd 28: *K2, P4, K6, P4, K2; rep from * another 5 (6, 7) times.

Rnd 29: *K2, P4, c3 over 3 left, P4, K2; rep from * another 5 (6, 7) times.

Rnd 30: *K2, P4, K6, P4, K2; rep from * another 5 (6, 7) times.

Rnd 31: *K2, P2, P2tog, K6, P2tog, P1, K2; rep from * another 5 (6, 7) times. 96 (112, 128) sts

Rnd 32: *K2, P3, K6, P3, K2; rep from * another 5 (6, 7) times.

Rnd 33: *Remove M, K2, PM, P3, K6, P3, K4; rep from * another 5 (6, 7) times.

Rnd 34: *P3, K1, SSK, K2tog, K1, P3, C2 over 2 Left; rep from * another 5 (6, 7) times. 84 (98, 112) sts

Rnd 35: *(P3, K4) twice; rep from * another 5 (6, 7) times.

Rnd 36: *(P1, P2tog, K4) twice; rep from * another 5 (6, 7) times. 72 (84, 96) sts

Rnd 37: *(P2, K4) twice; rep from * another 5 (6, 7) times.

Rnd 38: *(P2, K1, SKP, K1) twice; rep from * another 5 (6, 7) times. 60 (70, 80) sts

Rnd 39: *(P2tog, K3) twice; rep from * another 5 (6, 7) times. 48 (56, 64) sts.

Rnd 40: *(P1, K3): rep from * another 5 (6, 7) times.

Rnd 41: *(K2tog, K2) twice; rep from * another 5 (6, 7) times. 36 (42, 48) sts.

Rnd 42: *K4, K2tog; rep from * another 5 (6, 7) times. 30 (35, 40) sts.

Rnd 43: *K3, K2tog; rep from * another 5 (6, 7) times. 24 (28, 32) sts

Rnd 44: *K2, K2tog; rep from * another 5 (6, 7) times. 18 (21, 24) sts

Rnd 45: *K1, K2tog; rep from * another 5 (6, 7) times. 12 (14, 16) sts

Rnd 46: K2tog 6 (7, 8) times. 6 (7, 8) sts

Cut yarn and pull through remaining 6 (7, 8) sts.

Finishing

Weave in ends and lightly block as desired. Do no over block or hat will become too large.

Rooted Chart

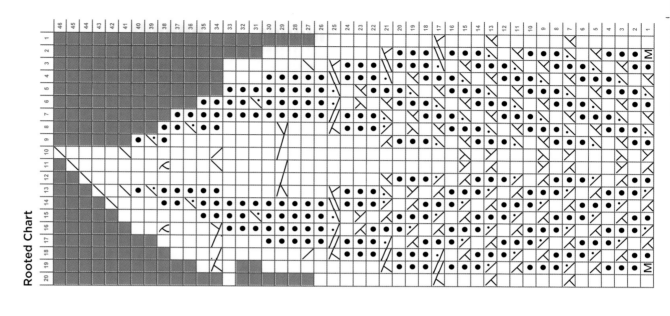

Legend

knit
knit stitch

make one
Make one by lifting strand in between stitch just worked and the next stitch, knit into back of this thread.

purl
purl stitch

Right Twist, purl bg
sl1 to CN, hold in back. k1, p1 from CN

Left Twist
sl1 to CN, hold in front. k1, k1 from CN

Left Twist, purl bg
sl1 to CN, hold in front. p1. k1 from CN

Right Twist
Skip the first stitch, knit into 2nd stitch, then knit skipped stitch. Slip both stitches from needle together OR k2tog leaving sts on LH needle, then k first st again, sl both sts off needle.

c1 over 2 right P
sl2 to CN, hold in back. k1, p2 from CN

c1 over 2 left P
sl 1 to CN, hold in front. p2, k1 from CN

No Stitch
Placeholder - No stitch made.

k2tog
Knit two stitches together as one stitch

ssk
Slip one stitch as if to knit, Slip another stitch as if to knit. Insert left-hand needle into front of these 2 stitches and knit them together

c3 over 3 left
sl3 to CN, hold in front. k3, k3 from CN

p2tog
Purl 2 stitches together

c2 over 2 left
sl 2 to CN, hold in front. k2, k2 from CN

sl1 k psso
slip 1, knit 1, pass slipped stitch over knit 1

Rooted Cable Hat   **31**

ZIGZAG MITTENS

by Emily Kintigh

FINISHED MEASUREMENTS

6.5 (7.5, 8.75)" hand circumference x 9.75
(11.25, 12.5)" total length

YARN

Knit Picks Swish Worsted (100% Superwash
Merino Wool; 110 yards/50g): MC Dove
Heather 25631, C1 Wonderland Heather
26067, C2 White 24662, C3 Carnation
24668, 1 ball each.

NEEDLES

US 6 (4mm) straight or circular needles and
DPNs, or size to obtain gauge.

US 4 (3.5mm) straight or circular needles, or
2 sizes smaller than gauge needle.

NOTIONS

Yarn Needle
Stitch Markers

GAUGE

22 sts and 24 rows = 4" on larger needles
over Zigzag Chart.

Zigzag Mittens

Notes:

The mittens are worked flat from the wrists up. The thumbs are worked separately and then sewn on during finishing. The chart is followed from bottom to top, knit RS rows (odd numbers) from right to left, and purl WS rows (even numbers) from left to right.

2x2 Ribbing (worked flat over multiples of 4 sts plus 2)
Row 1 (RS): K2, (P2, K2) to end.
Row 2 (WS): P2, (K2, P2) to end.
Repeat Rows 1-2 for pattern.

Stockinette Stitch (worked flat)
Row 1 (RS): K all sts.
Row 2 (WS): P all sts.
Repeat Rows 1-2 for pattern.

Stockinette Stitch (in the round)
All Rounds: K all sts.

MIL (Make 1 Left-leaning stitch)
PU the bar between st just worked and next st and place on LH needle as a regular stitch; knit through the back loop.

MIR (Make 1 Right-leaning stitch)
PU the bar between st just worked and next st and place on LH needle backwards (incorrect stitch mount). Knit through the front loop.

DIRECTIONS

Mitten

Cuff

With smaller needles and MC, loosely CO 38 (42, 50) sts. Work in 2x2 Ribbing until piece measures 3 (3.25, 3.5)" from CO edge ending with a WS row.

Size 7.5" Only: Inc 2 sts on last row of ribbing. 38 (44, 50) sts.

Switch to larger needles and begin working Zigzag Chart. Carry unused colors up the side of the mitten. Work all rows of chart 2 (3, 3) times, then repeat Rows 1-8 of chart 1 (0, 1) more time. Continuing remainder of Mitten with last used color, work 0 (2, 0) rows in St st.

Decrease Rows

Row 1 (RS): K1, (SSK, K2, K2tog) to last st, K1. 26 (30, 34) sts.
Row 2 (WS): P to end.
Row 3: K1, (SSK, K2tog) to last st, K1. 14 (16, 18) sts.
Row 4: P1, P2tog to last st, P1. 8 (9, 10) sts.

Cut yarn and pull through remaining sts.

Thumb

The thumbs are worked flat at first and are then joined in the round.

With larger needles and MC, loosely CO 3 sts.

Row 1 (WS): P to end.
Row 2 (RS): K1, M1L, K to last st, MIR, K1. 2 sts inc. 5 sts.
Row 3: P to end.

Repeat Rows 2-3 another 4 (5, 6) more times. 13 (15, 17) sts.
Next Row: K to end.

34 | ZigZag Mittens

Transfer sts to DPNs as follows: Place 4 (5, 6) sts on the first needle, 5 (5, 5) sts on the second needle and 4 (5, 6) sts on the third needle. PM and join in the round.

Working in St st, K 13 (15, 17) rnds.

Decrease Rounds

Size 6.5": K7, K2tog, K4. 12 sts. Then move on to Rnd 4 of decreases.

Size 7.5": Begin with Rnd 2 of decreases.

Size 8.75": Begin with Rnd 1 of decreases.

Rnd 1: K4, K2tog, K9, K2tog, 15 sts.
Rnd 2: (K3, K2tog) to end. 12 sts.
Rnd 3: K all sts.
Rnd 4: K2tog to end. 6 sts.

Cut yarn and pull through remaining sts.

Finishing

Using mattress stitch seaming, sew up the side of the mitten starting at the cuff, stopping 1 (1.25, 1.5)" past the cuff to place the thumb. Sew one side of the thumb to one side of the mitten, then the other side of the thumb to the other side of the mitten. Continue sewing the two sides together as before above the thumb up to the top of the mitten. Weave in ends, wash and block to measurements.

Zigzag Chart

Legend

☐	**knit** RS: knit stitch / WS: purl stitch
☐	C1
☐	C2
▨	C3

—— pattern repeat

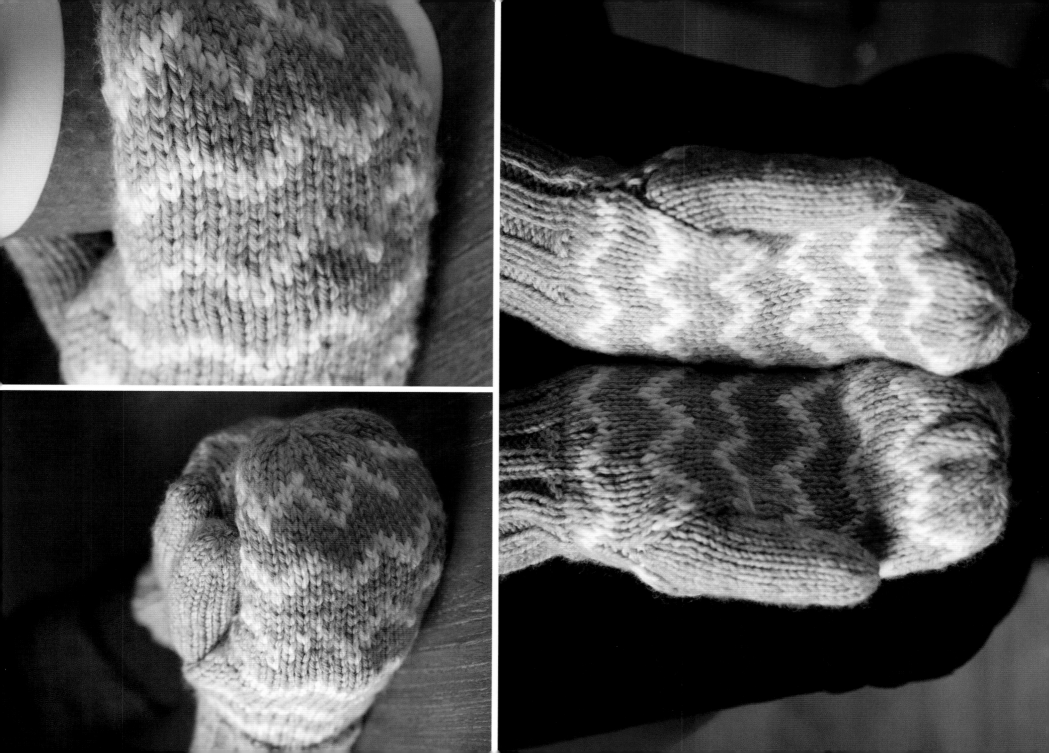

SUNSHINE DIAMOND WRAP

by Quenna Lee

FINISHED MEASUREMENTS

Approximately 61" long x 8" wide

YARN

Knit Picks Gloss Fingering (70% Merino Wool, 30% Silk; 220 yards/50g): MC Robot 25015, 2 balls; C1 Honey 25377, 1 ball.

NEEDLES

US 7 (4.5mm) 24" circular needles, or size to obtain gauge

NOTIONS

Scrap Yarn or Stitch Holder

Stitch Markers

Yarn Needle

GAUGE

20 sts and 32 rows = 4" over Seed Stitch and Diagonal Rib, blocked.

Three 6-st repeats of Diamond Slipped Stitch Pattern = 3" across x 2" high, blocked.

Sunshine Diamond Wrap

Notes:

The sample used exactly 2 skeins of the MC for maximum length, so if you are unsure of sufficient yardage, work fewer repeats of the Diagonal Rib pat after completion of the keyhole.

The center panel is worked flat in a slipped stitch pattern, alternating two colors. Using the main color, the side panels are worked with stitches picked up along the shorter ends of the center panel. The keyhole is formed by working right and left sides separately before joining to work in one piece again. Written and charted directions for the slipped stitch and diagonal rib patterns are provided. The charts are followed from right to left on RS rows (odd numbers) and left to right on WS rows (even numbers). Sl sts as if to purl WYIF.

Gathered Stitch: Insert needle under double strand of yarn, from front to back, K1, slip double strand over.

Seed Stitch Pattern (worked flat over an even number of sts)
Row 1(RS): *K1, P1; rep from * to end.
Row 2(WS): *P1, K1; rep from * to end.
Rep Rows 1-2 for pat.

Diamond Slip Stitch Pattern (worked flat in multiples of 6 sts)
Row 1 (RS, in MC): K3, (Sl 1 st)x3.
Rows 2 and 4 (WS): Purl in MC.
Row 3: Rep Row 1.
Row 5 (C1): (Sl 1 st)x3, K1, gathered st, K1.
Rows 6 and 8: Purl in C1.
Row 7 (C1): (Sl 1 st)x3, K3.
Row 9 (MC): K1, gathered st, K1, (Sl 1 st)x3.
Rows 10 and 12: Purl in MC.
Row 11: Rep Row 1.
Row 13: K4, gathered st, K1.
Row 14: Purl in MC.

Diagonal Rib Pattern (worked flat in multiples of 16 sts)
Row 1 (RS): (K2, P2)x2, (P2, K2)x2, (P2, K2)x2.
Row 2 (WS): (P2, K2)x2, (K2, P2)x2.
Row 3: K1, (P2, K2)x3, P2, K1.
Row 4: P1, (K2, P2)x3, K2, P1.
Row 5: Rep Row 2.
Row 6: Rep Row 1.
Row 7: P1, K2, P2, K6, P2, K2, P1.
Row 8: K1, P2, K2, P6, K2, P2, K1.
Rep Rows 1-8 for pat.

Right Diagonal Rib (worked flat over 24 sts)
Row 1 (RS): (K2, P2)x2, (P2, K2)x2, (P2, K2)x2.
Row 2 (WS): Sl 1 st, P1, K2, P2, K2, P2, K2, P1, K1 TBL.
Row 3: K1, (P2, K2)x3, P2 (P2, K2)x2, (K2, P2)x2.
Row 4: Sl 1 st, (K2, P2)x5, K2, P1.
Row 5: (P2, K2)x2, (K2, P2)x5, K2, P1.
Row 6: Sl 1 st, P1, K2, P2, K2, P2, K2, P1, K1 TBL.
Row 7: P1, K2, P2, K6, (K2, P2)x3, K1 TBL.
Row 8: Sl 1 st, P2, K2, P6, (K2, P2)x3, K1 TBL.
Rep Rows 1-8 for pat.

Left Diagonal Rib (worked flat over 24 sts)
Row 1 (RS): Sl 1 st, P1, K2, P2, K2, (K2, P2)x2, (P2, K2)x2.
Row 2 (WS): (P2, K2)x2, (K2, P2)x2, P2, K2, P1, K1.
Row 3: Sl 1 st, (P2, K2)x5, K2, P1.
Row 4: P1, (K2, P2)x5, K2, P1 TBL.
Row 5: Sl 1 st, K1, P2, K2, P2, (P2, K2)x2, (K2, P2)x2.
Row 6: (K2, P2)x2, (P2, K2)x2, P2, K2, P1, K1 TBL.
Row 7: Sl 1 st, (K2, P2)x3, K6, P2, K2, P1.
Row 8: K1, P2, K2, P6, (K2, P2)x3, K1 TBL.
Rep Rows 1-8 for pat.

DIRECTIONS

Center Panel

With MC, loosely CO 182 sts. Work Seed Stitch for 6 rows.

Diamond Slip Stitch
Row 1 (RS): Cont with MC, K1, work Row 1 of Diamond Slip Stitch pat to last st, K1.
Row 2 (WS): K1, work Row 2 of Diamond Slip Stitch pat to last st, K1.
Rows 3-4: Cont in pat, work Rows 3-4 of Diamond Slip Stitch pat.
Rows 5-8: Join C1, work Rows 5-8 of Diamond Slip Stitch pat.
Rows 9-12: Switch to MC, work Rows 9-12 of Diamond Slip Stitch pat.

Cont in pat, alternating between MC and C1 as indicated, until Rows 5-12 are worked 10 more times, ending after Row 12.

With MC, work Rows 13-14 once.

Work Seed Stitch for 6 rows.

BO loosely in pat.

Side Panel (make 2)

With RS facing up and MC, PU and K 52 sts along shorter edge.

Set Up Row (WS): Sl 1 st, P to last 2 sts, K1, K1 TBL.
Row 1 (RS): Sl 1 st, K1 work Diagonal Rib pat to last 2 sts, K1, K1 TBL.
Row 2: Sl 1 st, K1, cont in pat to last 2 sts, K1, K1 TBL.

Cont in pat until Rows 1-8 of Diagonal Rib pat are worked 3 times. Transfer last 26 sts for Left Keyhole to holder. 26 sts for Right Keyhole.

Right Keyhole
Row 1 (RS): Sl 1 st, K1 work Right Diagonal Rib pat.
Row 2 (WS): Cont Right Diagonal Rib pat to last 2 sts, K1, K1 TBL.

Rep last 2 rows, until Rows 1-8 of Right Diagonal Rib pat are worked 3 times, ending with a WS row. Transfer yarn to holder, do not cut yarn.

Left Keyhole
Transfer held sts to needle and join second ball of yarn, ready to work a RS row.
Row 1 (RS): Work Left Diagonal Rib pat to last 2 sts, K1, K1 TBL.
Row 2 (WS): Sl 1 st, K1, cont Left Diagonal Rib pat.

Rep last 2 rows until Rows 1-8 of Left Diagonal Rib pat are worked 3 times, ending with a WS row.

Break yarn. Transfer right sts to needle, in front of left sts, ready to work a RS row.

Next Row (RS): Sl 1 st, K1, cont Diagonal Rib pat to last 2 sts, K1, K1 TBL.

Next Row (WS): Sl 1 st, K1, cont Diagonal Rib pat to last 2 sts, K1, K1 TBL.

Rep last 2 rows until Rows 1-8 of Diagonal Rib pat are worked 6 times, ending with a WS row.

BO loosely in pat. Piece should measure 12" from the picked up edge after blocking.

Finishing

Weave in ends and block to measurements.

Legend

knit
RS: knit stitch
WS: purl stitch
□

purl
RS: purl stitch
WS: knit stitch
●

gathered stitch
insert needle under double strand of yarn, from front to back, k1, slip double strand over
∩

knit tbl
Knit stitch through back loop
B

slip wyif
Slip stitch as if to purl, with yarn in front
∨

C1

Diamond Rib Chart

Diamond Slipped Stitch Chart

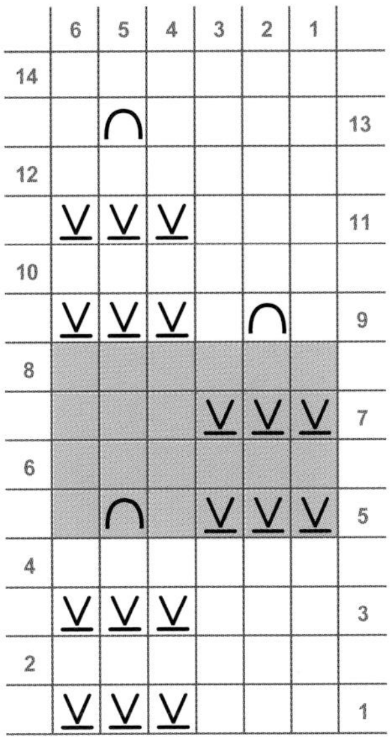

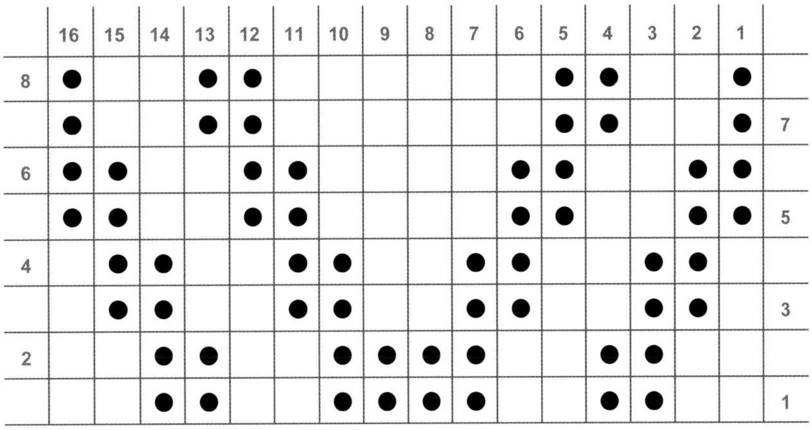

Right Diagonal Rib Chart

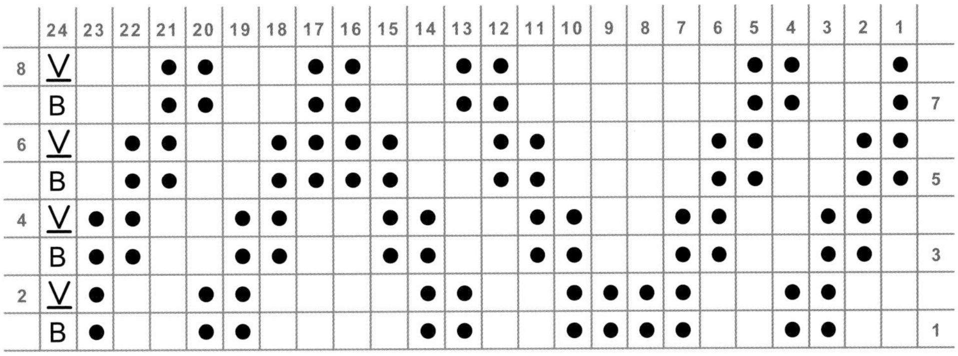

Left Diagonal Rib Chart

JULIET BAG

by Allison Griffith

FINISHED MEASUREMENTS

6" around x 4" high (approximate)

YARN

Knit Picks Stroll (75% Superwash Merino Wool, 25% Nylon; 231 yards/50g): MC White 26082, C2 Dandelion 25024, 1 ball each.

Knit Picks Stroll Brights (75% Superwash Merino Wool, 25% Nylon; 231 yards/50g): C1 Pucker 26401, 1 ball.

NEEDLES

US 2 (2.75mm) DPNs or two 24" circular needles for two circulars technique, or one 32" or longer circular needle for Magic Loop technique, or size to obtain gauge

NOTIONS

Yarn Needle
Stitch Marker

GAUGE

32 sts and 40 rounds = 4" in St st, in the round, blocked.

For pattern support, contact knittingontheneedles@gmail.com

Juliet Bag

Notes:

This tiny bag is worked in the round from the top down. Three variations of stripes and simple fair isle colorwork are charted for maximum stashbusting choice. Chart 3 was used for the pictured bag. The I-cord drawstring is knit separately, woven through the bag's eyelets, and the ends are grafted together for a seamless finish. The chart rows are followed from right to left, for all rounds.

I-Cord

*Knit a row. Slide row to other end of needle without turning work. Pull yarn firmly and repeat from *, creating a tube.

DIRECTIONS

Bag

The bag is worked in the round from the opening down.

With C1, loosely CO 48 sts and join in the round. PM for the beginning of the round.

Round 1: (K2, P2) around for 1 round. Break yarn and join MC.

Rounds 2-6: (K2, P2) around.

Round 7: (K2tog, YO, P2tog, YO) around.

Round 8: (K2, P2) around.

Rounds 9-10: K around.

Work Rounds 1-23 of Juliet Bag Chart 1, Juliet Bag Chart 2 or Juliet Bag Chart 3, knitting all stitches, and dropping and joining new colors of yarn as necessary.

With MC, K 2 rounds even.

Round 1: (K4, K2tog) around. 40 sts.

Round 2: K around.

Round 3: (K3, K2tog) around. 32 sts.

Round 4: K around.

Round 5: (K2, K2tog) around. 24 sts.

Round 6: K around.

Round 7: (K1, K2tog) around. 16 sts.

Round 8: K around.

Round 9: (K2tog) around. 8 sts.

Break yarn and pull through sts. Weave in end.

Drawstring

The drawstring is worked separately.

With C2, CO 3 sts, and set up to work I-cord. Knit I-cord until it measures 6.5". Break yarn, leaving a 10" tail.

With the I-cord still on the needles, weave the CO end through the eyelets of the bag. Then, carefully remove the live sts from the needle, and graft the two ends of the I-cord together.

Finishing

Weave in remaining ends, wash and block.

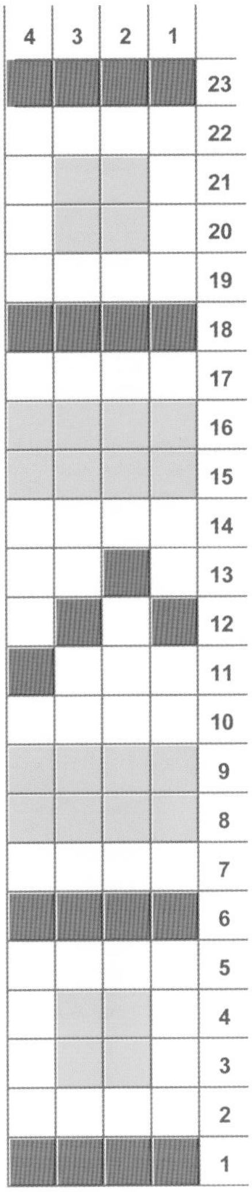

Chart 3

Legend

MC

C1

C2

Chart 2

Chart 1

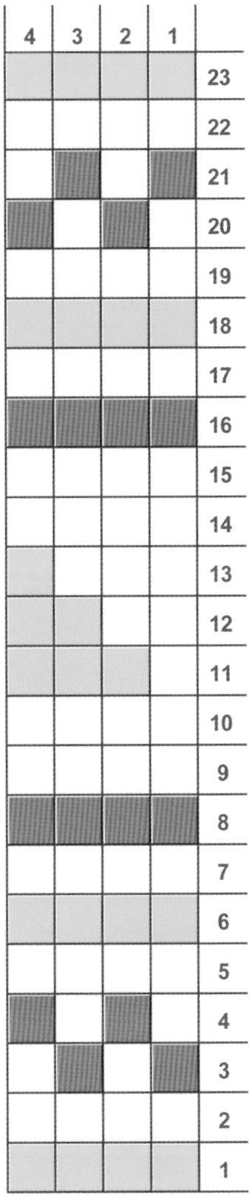

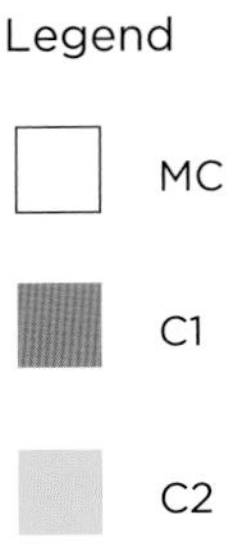

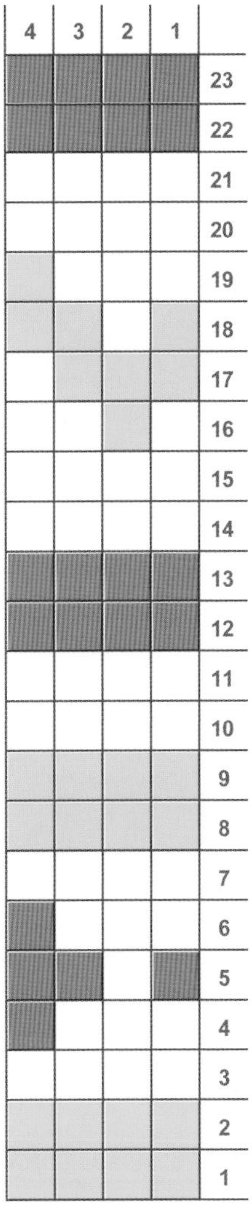

SIERRA MITTS

by Lynnette Hulse

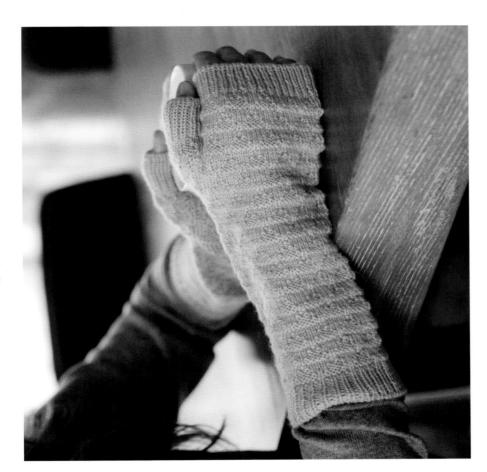

FINISHED MEASUREMENTS

5.5 (6, 6.5, 7.25)" circumference x 11.25" long, designed to have approximately 1.5" of ease.

YARN

Knit Picks Capretta (80% Fine Merino Wool, 10% Cashmere, 10% Nylon; 230 yards/50g): Solid Version: Sagebrush 26563, 2 balls.

Knit Picks Palette (100% Peruvian Highland Wool, 231 yards/50g): Striped Version: MC Cream 23730, C1 Caribbean 25095, C2 Turmeric 24251, 1 ball each.

NEEDLES

US 2 (2.75mm) DPNs or circular needles, or size to obtain gauge

Spare US 1 (2.25mm) DPNs or circular needles

NOTIONS

Yarn Needle

Stitch Markers

Scrap Yarn or Stitch Holder

GAUGE

40 sts and 48 rows = 4" in Stacked Triangles pattern in the round on larger needles, blocked lengthwise. (Gauge for this project is approximate)

Sierra Mitts

Notes:

These mitts feature a repeatable textured triangles pattern through both the main and thumb gusset areas. Knit bottom up, each mitt begins with a tubular cast on, and ends with a kitchenered tubular cast off for both the hand and thumb. The patterns for the textured triangles are in repeatable form, and in full for the thumb gusset and thumb top. All three are supplied in both charted and written form. The chart rows are followed from right to left, read as RS rows.

Stacked Triangles (in the round over multiples of 6 sts)
Rounds 1-2: *K1, P5; rep from * to end.
Rounds 3-4: *K2, P3, K1; rep from * to end.
Rounds 5-6: *K3, P1, K2; rep from * to end.
Rounds 7-8: *P3, K1, P2; rep from * to end.
Rounds 9-10: *P2, K3, P1; rep from * to end.
Rounds 11-12: *P1, K5; rep from * to end.
Repeat Rounds 1-12 for pattern.

Thumb Gusset (in the round over an even number of sts)
Round 1: K1, M1R, K1, M1L. 4 sts.
Round 2: K1, P2, K1.
Round 3: K1, M1R, P2, M1L, K1. 6 sts.
Round 4: K1, P3, K2.
Round 5: K1, M1R, P3, K1, M1L, K1. 8 sts.
Round 6: K3, P1, K4.
Round 7: K1, M1R, K2, P1, K3, M1L, K1. 10 sts.
Round 8: Knit.
Round 9: K1, M1R, P3, K1, P4, M1L, K1. 12 sts.
Round 10: *K1, P4* x2, P1, K1.
Round 11: K1, M1R, P3, K3, K1, M1L, K1. 14 sts.
Round 12: K2, *P3, K3* x2.
Round 13: K1, M1R, K2, P1, K5, P1, K3, M1L, K1. 16 sts.
Round 14: K4, *P1, K5* x2.
Round 15: K1, M1R, K14, M1L. 18 sts.
Round 16: K1, P4, *K1, P5* x2, K1.
Round 17: K1, M1R, P4, *K1, P5* x2, M1L, K1. 20 sts.
Round 18: K2, *P3, K3* x3.

Thumb Top (worked in the round over an even number of sts)
Round 1: K2, *P3, K3* x3, P2tog, P2, K2tog. 24 sts.
Rounds 2-3: K3, *P1, K5* x3, P1, K2.

Tubular Cast On
Step 1: Leaving a tail approximately three times the circumference of size working, make a slipknot and place it on the needle. Holding the needle in the right hand and both working yarn and tail in the left, insert the left thumb and index finger down in between the two strands, then turn your fingers back up, spreading them apart at the same time. The tail should now be wrapped around the thumb and the working yarn wrapped around your index finger.
Step 2: Bring the needle over the thumb strand, down under it, and up between the two strands.
Step 3: Bring the needle over the finger strand and back down beneath it.

Step 4: Bring the needle under the thumb strand and up, creating a knit st.
Step 5: Bring the needle over, behind, and under the index finger strand, and then forward and up between the two strands.
Step 6: Bring the needle over the thumb strand, down and back under both strands, bring the needle up to create a purl st on the needle.
Repeat steps 2-6 until you have the required number of sts, not counting the slipknot. Turn, wrap the tail counterclockwise around the working strand to secure the last st.

M2A (Make Two Away): Work a backwards loop CO twice, where the working yarn ends up pointing away from you. 2 sts inc.

M1L (Make 1 Left-leaning stitch)
PU the bar between st just worked and next st and place on LH needle as a regular stitch; K TBL.

M1R (Make 1 Right-leaning stitch)
PU the bar between st just worked and next st and place on LH needle backwards (incorrect stitch mount). K through the front loop.

DIRECTIONS
Cuff and Arm (make 2)

The cuff is initially worked flat then joined in the round after the second row.

Working flat on larger needles, using MC and Tubular Cast On, CO 54 (60, 66, 72) sts.
Row 1: *K1 TBL, Sl1 WYIF; rep from * to end.
Row 2: *K1, Sl1 WYIF; rep from * to end.
Join to work in the round, PM to indicate beginning of round.
Round 3: *K1, Sl1 WYIF; rep from * to end.
Round 4: *Sl1 WYIB, P1; rep from * to end.
Rounds 5-14: *K1, P1* to end.

Change to C1.
Round 15: Knit.
Rounds 16-33: Work 1.5 repeats of Stacked Triangles Chart (Rows 1-12 and then 1-6 again).

Change to MC.
Round 34: Knit.
Rounds 35-46: Work Rows 7-12 and then 1-6 of Stacked Triangles Chart.

Change to C1.
Round 47: Knit.
Rounds 48-65: Work 1.5 repeats of Stacked Triangles Chart, starting with Row 7 (Rows 7-12, then 1-12).

Change to MC.
Round 66: Knit.
Rounds 67-72: Work Rows 1-6 of Stacked Triangles Chart.

Change to C2.
Round 73: Knit.
Rounds 74-79: Work Rows 7-12 of Stacked Triangles Chart.

Change to MC.
Round 80: Knit.
Rounds 81-86: Work Rows 1-6 of Stacked Triangles Chart.

Thumb Gussets

Left Thumb Gusset

Change to C2.

Round 1: K1, PM, K1, M1R, K1, M1L, PM, K to end (Row 1 of Thumb Gusset Chart between markers).

Rounds 2-7: P1, SM, work Rows 2-7 of Thumb Gusset Chart between markers, SM, continue working Rows 7-12 of Stacked Triangles Chart as established.

Change to MC.

Round 8: K1, SM, K10 (Row 8 of Thumb Gusset Chart), SM, K to end.

Rounds 9-14: K1, SM, work Rows 9-14 of Thumb Gusset Chart between markers, SM, continue working Rows 1-6 of Stacked Triangles Chart as established.

Change to C2.

Round 15: K1, SM, K1, M1R, K14, M1L, K1 (Row 15 of Thumb Gusset Chart), SM, K to end.

Rounds 16-18: P1, SM, work Rows 16-18 of Thumb Gusset Chart between markers, SM, continue working Rows 7-9 of Stacked Triangles Chart as established. 20 gusset sts, 72 (78, 84, 90) sts total.

Round 19: P1, remove M, transfer 20 gusset sts to stitch holder or waste yarn, remove M, M2A, continue working Stacked Triangles Chart as established. 54 (60, 66, 72) sts.

Right Thumb Gusset

Change to C2.

Round 1: K to 2 sts from end of round, PM, K1, M1R, K1, M1L, K1 (Row 1 of Thumb Gusset Chart between markers).

Rounds 2-7: Work Rows 7-12 of Stacked Triangles Chart as established until first M, SM, work Rows 2-7 of Thumb Gusset Chart between markers.

Change to MC.

Round 8: K to M, SM, K10 (Row 8 of Thumb Gusset Chart).

Rounds 9-14: Work Rows 1-6 of Stacked Triangles Chart to M, SM, work Rows 9-14 of Thumb Gusset Chart.

Change to C2.

Round 15: K to M, SM, K1, M1R, K14, M1L, K1 (Row 15 of Thumb Gusset Chart).

Rounds 16-18: Work Rows 7-9 of Stacked Triangles Chart to M, SM, work Rows 16-18 of Thumb Gusset Chart. 20 gusset sts, 72 (78, 84, 90) sts total.

Round 19: Continue working Stacked Triangles Chart as established until M, M2A, remove M, transfer 20 sts to stitch holder or waste yarn. 54 (60, 66, 72) sts.

Hand

Continuing in C2:

Rounds 1-2: Work Rows 11-12 of Stacked Triangles Chart as established 54 (60, 66, 72) sts.

Change to MC.

Round 3: Knit.

Round 4-9: Work Rows 1-6 of Stacked Triangles Chart.

Change to C2.

Round 10: Knit.

Round 11-16: Work Rows 7-12 of Stacked Triangles Chart.

Change to MC.

Round 17: Knit.

Round 18-27: *K1, P1* to end.

Round 28: Rep *K1, SL1 WYIF* to end.

Round 29: Rep *SL1 WYIB, P1* to end.

Round 30-31: Repeat Rounds 28-29.

Break yarn leaving a tail approximately three times the circumference of work. With second smaller circular needles or DPNs readied, slip all knit sts to the working needle and all purl stitches to the second set to separate them. Thread the tail through a tapestry needle. Kitchener stitch the separated sts closed.

Thumb

Transfer sts from waste yarn to needles, PU 6 sts from the CO edge. PM to denote beginning/end of round. 26 sts.

Continuing in C2:

Round 1: Work Round 1 of Thumb Top Chart. 24 sts.

Rounds 2-3: Work Rounds 2-3 of Thumb Top Chart.

Change to MC.

Round 4: Knit.

Round 5-14: *K1, P1* to end.

Round 15: *K1, SL1 WYIF; rep from * to end.

Round 16: *SL1 WYIB, P1; rep from * to end.

Round 17-18: Repeat Rounds 15-16.

As with top of Hand; break yarn leaving a tail approximately three times the circumference of work. With second smaller circular needles or DPNs readied, slip all knit sts to the working needle and all purl sts to the second set to separate them. Thread the tail through a tapestry needle, Kitchener stitch the separated sts closed.

Finishing

Weave in all ends, using the CO tail to close off tiny gap found at area worked flat at beginning of project. Block mitt lengthwise only.

Stacked Triangles Chart

	6	5	4	3	2	1
12						•
11						•
10	•	•			•	•
9	•	•			•	•
8	•	•	•	•	•	•
7	•	•	•	•	•	•
6			•			
5			•			
4	•		•	•		
3	•	•	•	•		
2	•	•	•	•	•	•
1	•	•	•	•	•	•

Legend

□ **knit**
knit stitch

• **purl**
purl stitch

▨ **no stitch**
Placeholder - No stitch made.

 make one right
Place a firm backward loop over the right needle, so that the yarn end goes towards the back

 make one left
Place a firm backward loop over the right needle, so that the yarn end goes towards the front

p2tog
Purl 2 stitches together

k2tog
Knit two stitches together

Thumb Gusset Chart

	18	17	16	15	14	13	12	11	10	9	8	7	6	5	4	3	2	1
1																		
2		MR																
3	●	●	●	MR														
4	●	●	●			MR												
5	●	●	●					MR										
6		●	●				●	●	●	MR								
7					●	●	●	●	●	●		MR						
8		●	●				●	●	●	●				MR				
9	●	●	●					●	●					●	●	MR		
10	●	●	●									●	●	●	●	●	●	MR
11	●	●	●						●	●				●	●	●	●	
12		●	●				●	●	●	●						ML		ML
13					●	●	●	●	●	●				ML				
14		●	●				●	●	●	●		ML						
15	●	●	●						●	ML								
16	●	●	●				ML											
17	●	●	●			ML												
18		●	●	ML														
19	ML																	
20																		

Thumb Top Chart

	3	2	1
1			
2			
3			●
4	●	●	●
5			●
6			
7			
8			
9			●
10	●	●	●
11			●
12			
13			
14			
15			●
16	●	●	●
17			●
18			
19			
20			
21			/
22	●	●	●
23		●	
24			/

NEW YORK COWL

by Trelly Hernández

FINISHED MEASUREMENTS

19" (48.5cm) circumference x 16" (40cm) high

YARN

Knit Picks Stroll (75% Superwash Merino, 25% Nylon; 231 yards/50g):
C1 White 26082, C2 Black 23701, C3 Dandelion 25024, 1 ball each.

NEEDLES

US 2.5 (3mm) 16" circular needles, or size to obtain gauge.

NOTIONS

Yarn Needle
Stitch Markers
Cable Needle

GAUGE

32 sts and 37 rnds = 4" in stranded St st in the round, blocked.

New York Cowl

Notes:

Squares, stripes, and yarn overs result in an adorable cowl reminiscent of a New York taxi cab.

When working the charts, read all rows from right to left as if a RS row.

C4F Cable: Sl 2 sts from left needle to CN and hold at front, K2 sts from left needle. K2 from CN.

DIRECTIONS

Using the Long Tail Cast On and C1, CO 152 sts, PM and join in the round being careful not to twist your sts.

Ribbing Round: *K1 TBL, P1, rep from * to end.
Work 14 Ribbing Rounds.

Work Chart Section 1, working sts 1-8 19 times across the rnd, and repeating Rnds 1-8 a total of 5 times.
Work Chart Section 2, working Rnds 1-28 once, then repeating Rnds 1-12 once more.
Work Chart Section 3, working Rnds 1-34 once, then repeating Rnds 1-6 once more.
With C1, work the Ribbing Round for 14 rounds again. Bind off.

Finishing

Weave in ends, wash and block.

Section 1 Chart

	8	7	6	5	4	3	2	1
1	●		●			■		
2		●				■	●	
3	●		●			■		
4		●				■		
5	●		●			■		
6		●				■		
7	●		●			■		
8		●				■	●	

Legend

knit
knit stitch

purl
purl stitch

yo
yarn over

k2tog
knit two stitches together as one stitch

slkpsso
slip 1, knit 1, pass slipped stitch over knit st

c4f
sl 2 to CN, hold in front. k2. k2 from CN

C1

C2

C3

Section 2 Chart

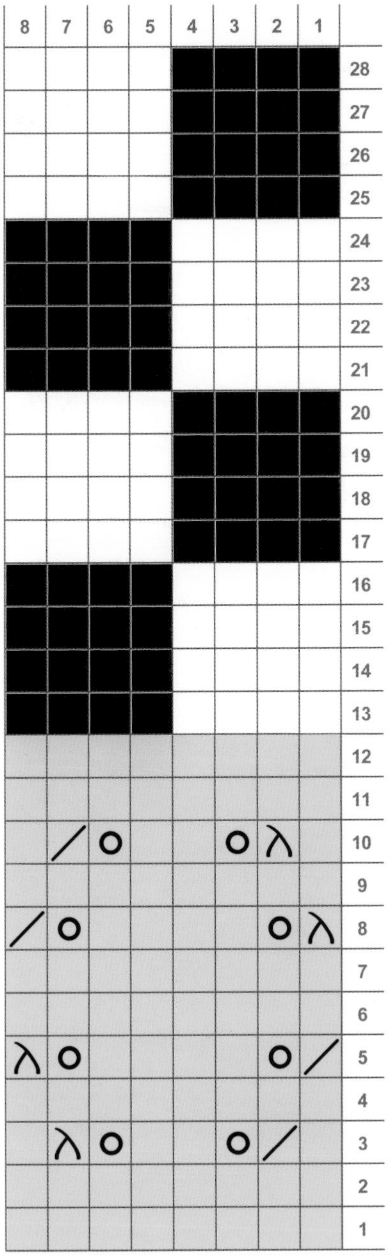

Section 3 Chart

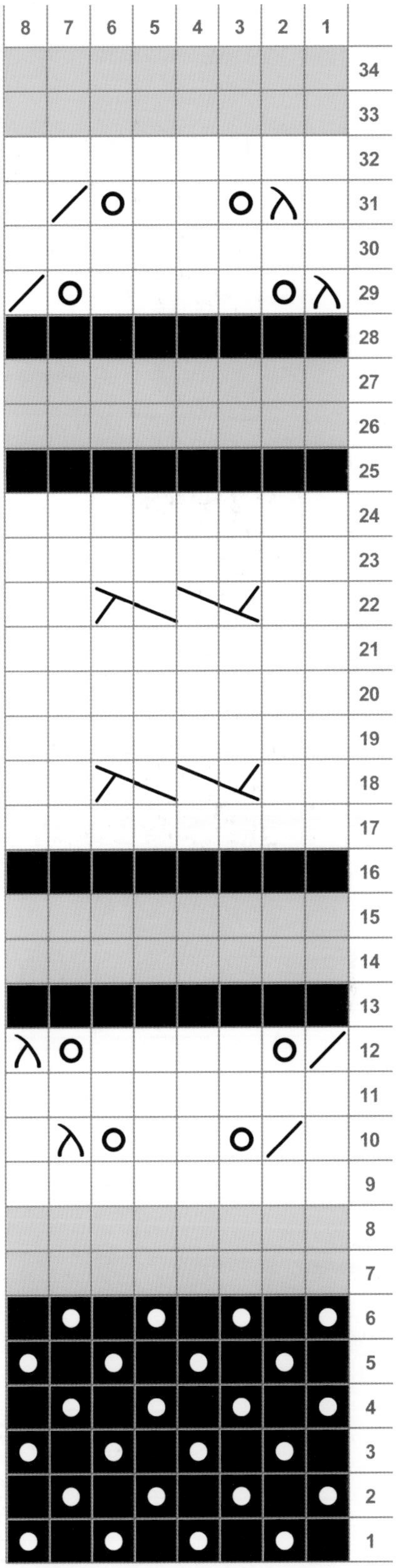

SWELL HAT

by Tetiana Otruta

FINISHED MEASUREMENTS

Small (Medium, Large) 20 (22, 24)" circumference; to fit 20–21 (21.5–22.5, 23–24)" / 51–53.5 (54–57, 58–61)cm head circumference.

7.25 (7.5, 7.75)"/18.5 (19, 19.5)cm Beanie length; 8.75 (9, 9.25)"/22.5 (23, 23.5)cm Slouchy length.

YARN

Knit Picks Capretta (80% Fine Merino Wool, 10% Cashmere, 10% Nylon; 230 yards/50g):

MC Cream 25600, C1 Harbor 25598, 1 ball each.

NEEDLES

US 1 (2.5mm) DPNs or two 24" circular needles for two circulars technique, or one 32" or longer circular needle for Magic Loop technique, or size to obtain gauge.

US 3 (3.25 mm) DPNs or two 24" circular needles for two circulars technique, or one 32" or longer circular needle for Magic Loop technique, or size to obtain gauge.

NOTIONS

Stitch Markers (one marker in different color for rnd beginning)

Yarn Needle

Pom-Pom maker (optional)

GAUGE

30 sts and 36 rnds = 4" in stranded Colorwork pattern in the round on larger needle, blocked.

32 sts and 40 rnds = 4" in St st in the round on smaller needle, blocked.

For pattern support, contact tetianaotruta@gmail.com

Swell Hat

Notes:

The Swell Hat is worked in the round. Read Chart A from right to left. The number of repeats for the Medium and Large size hats are written in parentheses where different.

The last stitch of the round in the Colorwork section is not shown on the chart or in the written line-by-line instructions. Purl with MC this last stitch in the round, to balance gap in colorwork pattern at the beginning and the end of the rnd.

1x1 Rib (worked in the round over multiples of 2 sts)
Rnd 1: (K1, P1) around.
Repeat Rnd 1 for patt.

Colorwork pattern, Chart A (worked in the round over 15 sts)
Rnd 1: K1 C1, K2 MC, K3 C1, K4 MC, K3 C1, K2 MC.
Rnds 2-3: K1 MC, K2 C1, K3 MC, K4 C1, K3 MC, K2 C1.
Rnds 4-6: Rep Rnd 1.
Rnds 7-10: Rep Rnd 2.
Rnds 11-13: Rep Rnd 1.
Rnds 14-15: Rep Rnd 2.
Rep Rnds 1-15 for patt.

DIRECTIONS
Hat

With smaller needles loosely CO 130 (140, 154) sts with MC. Join sts in the round and PM for rnd beginning, being careful not to twist sts.

Work 14 rnds of 1x1 Rib in the round.

Increase Rnd
Small: K3, M1, K7, M1, *K6, M1, K7, M1; rep from * 9 times, K to end, M1 P-wise. 151 sts.
Medium: K3, M1, *K5, M1, K6, M1; rep from * 12 times, K to end, M1 P-wise. 166 sts.
Large: K3, *K5, M1, K6, M1; rep from * 13 times, K to end, M1 P-wise. 181 sts.

Switch to larger needles.

Work Colorwork pattern Rnd 1 over 150 (165, 180) sts using Chart A or written instructions 10 (11, 12) times around to last st, P1 MC.

Note: You may use additional stitch markers for every Colorwork pattern repeat.

Continue as established, working Rnds 1-15 of Chart A a total of 2 times for Beanie length and 3 times for Slouchy length. Then, work Rnd 1 of Chart A once.

Break C1, work the remainder of the hat in MC. Remove all additional markers if you used them, except beginning of rnd.

Switch to smaller needles.

Next Rnd: K to 2 sts from end of the rnd. SKP. 150 (165, 180) sts.
Transition Rnd: K12 (16, 20), *SKP, K23 (31, 43); rep from * 5 (4, 3) times. SKP, K to end. 144 (160, 176) sts.

Work Crown shaping for either Beanie or Slouchy length, then continue to Finishing.

Crown Shaping, Beanie length
Rnd 1: *SKP, K16 (18, 20), PM; repeat from * to end of rnd. 136 (152, 168) sts.
Rnd 2: Knit.
Rnd 3: *SKP, K to M, SM; repeat from * to end of rnd. 128 (144, 160) sts.
Repeat Rnds 2-3, 14 (16, 18) times more. 16 sts.
Repeat Rnd 3 once. 8 sts.

Crown Shaping, Slouchy length
Rnd 1: *SKP, K16 (18, 20), PM; repeat from * to end of rnd. 136 (152, 168) sts.
Rnd 2: Knit.
Rnd 3: *SKP, K to M, SM; repeat from * to end of rnd. 128 (144, 160) sts.
Rnd 4: *SKP, K to M, SM; repeat from * to end of rnd. 120 (136, 152) sts.
Repeat Rnds 2-4, 5 (5, 6) times more. 40 (56, 56) sts.
Repeat Rnd 3, 4 (6, 6) times. 8 sts.

Finishing
Cut the yarn leaving an 6" tail. Draw the yarn tail through the remaining 8 sts with yarn needle and pull to close top of hat.

Weave in ends and block hat.

Make about 2" diameter pom-pom with C1 and attach to top of hat (optional).

Chart A

Legend

knit
knit stitch

MC

C1

CASA LOMA SHAWL

by Brenda Castiel

FINISHED MEASUREMENTS

55" wide x 14" deep at widest point after blocking, relaxed

YARN

Knit Picks Galileo (50% Merino Wool, 50% Viscose from Bamboo; 131 yards/50g): Urchin 26575, 3 balls.

NEEDLES

US 6 (4.0mm) straight or circular needles, or size to obtain gauge

NOTIONS

Yarn Needle
Stitch Markers

GAUGE

20 sts and 28 rows = 4" in Garter St, blocked. (Gauge for this project is approximate)

For pattern support, contact BCASTIEL@yahoo.com

Casa Loma Shawl

Notes:

Casa Loma is a long triangular shawlette or scarf that is just the right length to wrap around the neck once. Garter stitch is knit to a looser gauge to create a soft, cushy fabric that drapes nicely. The lacy edge provides interest and charm. This shawlette can take you through all of the seasons. The shape and weight are ideal to wear underneath a coat - the tapered ends can be tucked in to look like a cowl.

It is knit side to side, from one point to the other.

If you have more yarn, and you want to knit a larger shawl, weigh your yarn, and work until half your yarn plus 10% remains, then start Part 2 (e.g. if you have 150 grams, work Part 1 until 75+15 or 90 grams are left, then start Part 2).

Make 1 into 7

[(K1, YO) 3 times, K1] into same st. 6 sts inc.

S2kp

Sl 2 sts K-wise, K1, PSSO. 2 sts dec.

DIRECTIONS

Part 1

Cast on 3 sts.

Row 1 (RS): KFB, K to end. 4 sts.

Row 2 (WS): Knit.

Row 3: Repeat Row 1. 5 sts.

Row 4: Knit.

Row 5: KFB, K until 4 sts remain, K2tog, YO, K2. 6 sts.

Rows 6-11: Repeat Rows 4-5, 3 times. 9 sts.

Row 12: Knit.

Row 13: KFB, K2, YO, K2tog, K until 4 sts remain, K2tog, YO, K2. 10 sts.

Row 14: Knit.

Rows 15-30: Repeat Rows 13-14 8 more times. 18 sts.

Row 31: Work Lace Chart (Row 1), PM, K2, YO, K to last 4 sts, PM, K2tog, YO, K2. 25 sts.

Row 32: K to second marker, work Lace Chart (Row 2).

Row 33: Work Lace Chart (Row 3), SM, K2, YO, K to marker, SM, K2tog, YO, K2. 26 sts.

Repeat Rows 32-33, continuing to work the Lace Chart as established, working a total of 9 repeats of the Chart (ending with Row 12). 72 sts.

Part 2

Note: At this point the triangle shape stops increasing and is worked even for 4 repeats.

Row 1 (RS): Work Lace Chart (Row 1), SM, K2, YO, K2tog, K to marker, SM, K2tog, YO, K2. 78 sts.

Row 2 (WS): K to second marker, work Lace Chart (Row 2).

Repeat Rows 1-2, continuing to work the Lace Chart as established, working 4 repeats of the Chart (ending with Row 12). 72 sts.

Part 3

Note: At this point the triangle shape begins decreasing.

Row 1 (RS): Work Lace Chart (Row 1), SM, K2, YO, K3tog, K to marker, SM, K2tog, YO, K2. 77 sts.

Row 2 (WS): K to second marker, work Lace Chart (Row 2).

Repeat Rows 1-2, working 9 repeats of the Lace Chart. 18 sts.

You may remove markers.

Row 109: K1, YO, K2tog, YO, K3tog, K to last 4 sts, K2tog, YO, K2. 17 sts.

Row 110: Knit.

Rows 111-124: Repeat Rows 109-110 7 more times. 10 sts.

Row 125: K1, YO, K2tog, YO, K3tog, YO, K2. 9 sts.

Row 126: Knit.

Row 127: K1, K2tog, YO, K2tog, K2tog, YO, K2. 8 sts.

Row 128: Knit.

Row 129: K2, K2tog, K2tog, YO, K2. 7 sts.

Row 130: Knit.

Row 131: K1, K2tog, K2tog, YO, K2. 6 sts.

Row 132: Knit.

Row 133: K2tog, K2tog, YO, K2. 5 sts.

Row 134: Knit.

Row 135: K1, K2tog, K2. 4 sts.

Row 136: Knit.

Row 137: K2tog, K2. 3 sts.

BO remaining sts.

Finishing

Weave in ends, wash and block to Finished Measurements into gentle triangle shape to open up lace design. Block edging into rounded motifs.

Lace Chart

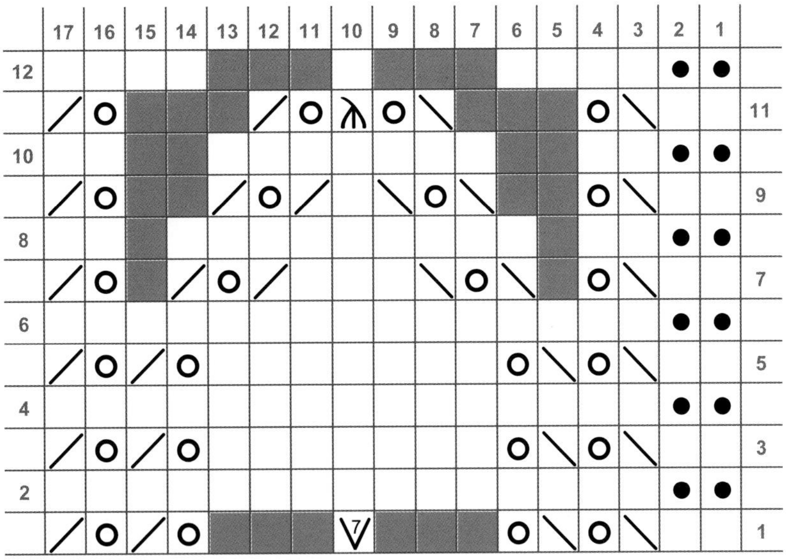

RS rows (odd numbers) are worked from right to left, WS rows (even numbers) are worked left to right.

Legend

knit
RS: knit stitch
WS: purl stitch

ssk
RS: Slip one stitch as if to knit, Slip another stitch as if to knit. Insert left-hand needle into front of these 2 stitches and knit them together
WS: Purl two stitches together in back loops, inserting needle from the left, behind and into the backs of the 2nd & 1st stitches in that order

yo
RS: Yarn Over

No Stitch
RS: Placeholder - No stitch made.

m7 sts in one
[(K1, YO) 3 times, K1] into same st. 6 sts inc.

k2tog
RS: Knit two stitches together as one stitch
WS: Purl 2 stitches together

purl
RS: purl stitch
WS: knit stitch

sl1 k2tog psso
Sl 2 sts K-wise, K1, pass the two slipped sts over. 2 sts dec.

MOLLY'S HAT

by Linda Riley

FINISHED MEASUREMENTS

16 (20, 24)" circumference, to fit Toddler (Adult Medium, Adult, Large)

YARN

Knit Picks Brava Bulky (100% Premium Acrylic; 136 yards/100g):

Tranquil 25740 (C1), Canary 25736 (C2), White 25724 (C3), 1 ball each

NEEDLES

US 9 (5.5 mm) DPN or circular needles, or size needed to obtain gauge

NOTIONS

Stitch markers

Yarn Needle

Pom Pom Maker (Optional)

GAUGE

16 stitches and 23 rows = 4" stockinette stitch, blocked

For pattern support, contact linda.c.riley@gmail.com

Molly's Hat

Notes:

This hat is knitted in the round using stranded technique for the color work. It features a ribbed brim intended to be turned up.

The body of the hat is knit in stockinette stitch. Refer to Color Chart for color work.

DIRECTIONS

Brim

With C1, CO 64 (80, 96) stitches. Join in the round.

Round 1: (K2, P2) to end.

Repeat Round 1 for 8 (10, 10) rounds total.

Body

Using C1, knit for 10 (12, 12) rounds

Work Color Chart over next 14 (15, 15) rounds, following the directions for your chosen size.

Using C3, knit for 2 (3, 4) rounds

Crown Decreases

Setup Round: Knit next round, placing stitch marker every 16 (16, 16) stitches. Total of 4 (5, 6) markers

Round 1: (K1, SSK, K until 3 sts before marker, K2tog, K1, SM) repeat 3 (4, 5) times

Round 2: Knit

Repeat rounds 1-2 until 16 (20, 24) stitches remain

Round 13: K2tog 8 (10, 12) times

Final Round: K2tog 4 (5, 6) times

Finishing

Cut yarn leaving 10 inch tail. Using yarn needle, weave tail through remaining stitches and pull tightly. Turn hat inside and weave in end. Weave in all other loose ends.

Pom Pom

Make large pom pom using a pom pom maker or the following technique:

Using C3, wrap repeatedly around three fingers on one hand. Cut yarn. Remove from fingers and place flat onto work surface. Cut another 12 in piece of yarn. Tie 12 inch piece tightly around the center of main poof. Cut ends of poof loops. Trim all strands until an even pom pom is achieved.

Place on top of hat and weave ends from 12 in piece into hat, securing tightly.

Color Chart

Legend

knit
knit stitch

C1

C2

C3

Toddler Size- repeat 4x per rnd

Adult Medium and Large- repeat 5 (6)x per rnd

DAISY SLIPPERS

by Amanda Lilley

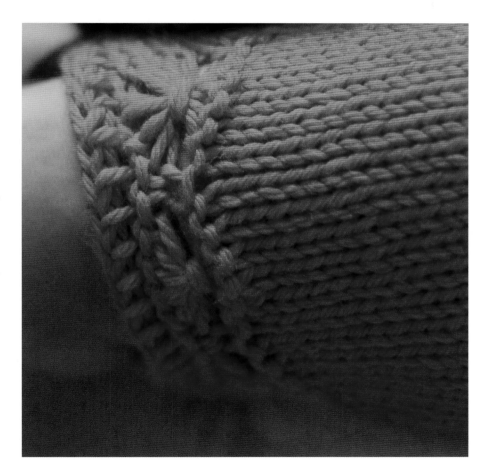

FINISHED MEASUREMENTS

8" to 9" foot circumference (measurement taken around the ball of the foot), length is adjustable.

YARN

Knit Picks Swish Worsted Brights (100% Superwash Merino Wool; 110 yards/ 50g): Pucker 26639, 2 balls.

NEEDLES

US 5 (3.75mm) DPNs or longer circular needle for Magic Loop technique, or size to obtain gauge

US 7 (4.5mm) DPNs, or 2 sizes larger than gauge needle

NOTIONS

Yarn Needle
Stitch Markers

GAUGE

20 sts and 28 rows = 4" in St st in the round on smaller needles, blocked.

For pattern support, contact Amandalilleydesigns@yahoo.com

Daisy Slippers

Notes:

The Daisy Slippers are knit from the toe up and feature a feminine daisy pattern across the top instep, a short row heel, and an I-cord bind off.

Make 1 Right (M1R): Use LH needle to lift the horizontal strand between the two needles from back to front, K into the front of the lifted strand.

Make 1 Left (M1L): Use LH needle to lift the horizontal strand between needles from front to back, K into the back of the lifted strand.

Wrap and Turn (W&T)
Slip next st to RH needle, yarn forward between needles, Sl st back to LH needle, yarn back. Turn work.
Hiding the wraps: Work to the wrapped st. For RS rows, lift the wrap over the wrapped st, K the wrap and the st together TBL. On WS rows, lift the wrap over the wrapped st and P the wrap and the wrapped st tog.

Daisy Stitch
*Sl next st dropping the 2 extra wraps; rep from * 5 times, **bring yarn forward between needles, Sl 5 sts back to left needle, bring yarn back between needles, Sl 5 sts to right needle; rep from ** twice.

DIRECTIONS

Using smaller circular needle CO 26 sts using Judy Becker's Magic Cast on. http://www.youtube.com/watch?v=1pmxRDZ-cwo.

Round 1: K.

Round 2: *K1, M1R, K11, M1L, K1; rep from * twice. 30 sts.

Rounds 3 through 5: K.

Round 6: *K1, M1R, K13, M1L, K1; rep from * twice. 34 sts.

Rounds 7 through 9: K.

Round 10: *K1, M1R, K15, M1L, K1; rep from * twice 38 sts.

Continue to knit in the round until slipper measures 4.75" from CO.

Begin Instep Pattern

Round 1: P 19 sts for instep, K to end of round.

Round 2: *K1 (K1 wrapping yarn 3 times around needle, instead of once, before pulling through st) 5 times; repeat from * twice, K to end of round.

Round 3: K1, *work Daisy Stitch over 5 sts, K1; rep from * 3 times, K to end of round.

Round 4: K.

K4 sts, BO next 11 sts P-wise, K across remaining sts but do not stop at the beginning of the round, continue to knit the 4 sts that remain on the front needle. 27 sts.

From this point you will be working back and forth in rows.

Row 1 (WS): Sl 1, P to end of row.

Row 2 (RS): Sl 1, K to end of row.

Repeat last 2 rows until slipper measures 7.5" from CO, or 1" short of desired length to back heel. End after finishing a WS row.

Heel Turn

Row 1 (RS): Sl 1, K5, PM, K14, W&T.

Row 2 (WS): P13, W&T.

Row 3: K11, W&T.

Row 4: P to 9 sts, W&T.

Row 5: K7, W&T.

Row 6: P5, W&T.

Row 7: K10 sts, hiding all wraps as you come to them. W&T.

Row 8: P to M, hiding all wraps as you come to them. Remove M, W&T.

Row 9: K to 1 st before wrapped st, work a SSK hiding the wrap. Turn.

Row 10: Sl 1 P-wise, P to 1 st before wrapped st, P2tog hiding wrap. (This requires you to slip the first st to your RH needle, lift the wrap over the wrapped st and leave it on the LH needle, return the slipped st back to the LH needle and P2tog (3 together if you count the wrap) to hide the wrap. Turn.

Row 11: Sl 1, K13, SSK, turn.

Row 12: Sl 1, P13, P2tog, turn.

Repeat Rows 11-12, 4 more times until 15 sts remain.

Next Row (RS): K across 15 sts, PU and K 1 in each st along the inside of the foot, across the instep, and along the outside (the number of sts picked up will vary by the length of the slipper). Join to work in the round.

Applied I-cord

Work an applied I-cord using larger needle across all sts.

Applied I-cord: *K2, K2tog TBL, replace these 3 sts back onto LH needle. Pull yarn across the back of the three sts and repeat from * to the end of the round. You will have 3 sts on RH needle, Sl the second and third st over the first st on the needle.

Finishing

Draw yarn through, cut and weave in ends, block to measurements.

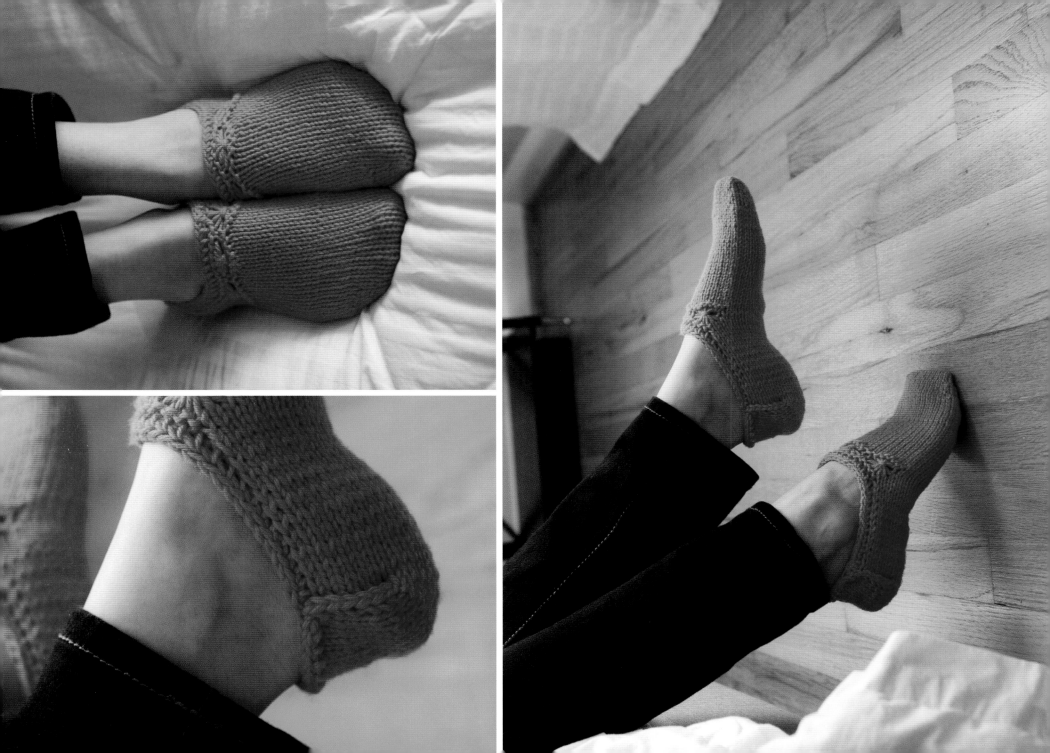

WINTER BLOOMS

by Stephannie Tallent

FINISHED MEASUREMENTS

6 (8)" palm circumference

YARN

Knit Picks Palette (100% Peruvian Highland Wool; 231 yards/50g): MC Oyster Heather 24559, C1 Peony 25093, C2 Semolina 24250, C3 Black 23729, 1 ball each.

NEEDLES

US 1 (2.25mm) DPNs or two 24" circular needles for two circulars technique, or one 32" or longer circular needle for Magic Loop technique, or size to obtain gauge

NOTIONS

Yarn Needle

Stitch Markers

Scrap Yarn or Stitch Holder

Crochet Hook or as preferred for Provisional CO

GAUGE

32 sts and 48 rnds = 4" in St st in the round, blocked.

For pattern support, contact stephannie@sunsetcat.com

Winter Blooms

Notes:

These mittens are worked from the cuff up in the round. Use the provisional cast on of your choice to cast on; these stitches will be joined to the live stitches to form the picot hem of the cuff. Work the background flower color chart in stranded St st; additional colors are duplicate stitched after the mitten is finished and blocked. The thumb gusset is formed by right and left lifted increases. The top of the mitten is grafted with Kitchener stitch.

Right Lifted Increase (RLI):

Insert your right needle into the stitch below the next stitch on your left needle. Knit this stitch, then insert your needle into the next stitch on the needle (the one above the stitch you just knit) and knit.

Left Lifted Increase (LLI):

Use your left needle to pick up the stitch that is two stitches below the first stitch on the right needle (the last stitch you made). Knit this stitch through the back loop.

Kitchener Stitch

With an equal number of sts on two needles, break yarn leaving a long tail and thread through yarn needle. Hold needles parallel, with WS's facing in and both needles pointing to the right. Perform Step 2 on the first front st, and then Step 4 on the first back st, and then continue with instructions below.

1: Pull yarn needle K-wise through front st and drop st from knitting needle.

2: Pull yarn needle P-wise through next front st, leave st on knitting needle.

3: Pull yarn needle P-wise through first back st and drop st from knitting needle.

4: Pull yarn needle K-wise through next back st, leave st on knitting needle.

Repeat steps 1-4 until all sts have been grafted.

DIRECTIONS

Cuff

Picot Hem

Using MC and the provisional cast on of your choice, CO 48 (64) sts. Join to work in the round, being careful not to twist. PM for beginning of round.

Change to C1 and knit 10 rnds.

Next Rnd: (K2tog, yo) to end.

Change to MC. Knit 10 rnds.

Joining Rnd: Place provisionally CO sts onto a second needle. Fold WS of hem together. *K2tog, using 1 st from front needle (live sts) and 1 st from back needle (provisionally CO sts). Repeat from * to end.

Knit 2 rnds.

Cuff Chart

Work Rows 1-21 of the Cuff chart for your size, twice around.

Knit 1 rnd.

Main Body

Gusset Increases

Setup Rnd, Left Mitt: K21 (29) sts, PM for gusset, K2, PM for gusset, K to end.

Setup Rnd, Right Mitt: K25 (33) sts, PM for gusset, K2, PM for gusset, K to end.

Rnd 1: K to gusset marker, SM, RLI, K to second gusset marker, LLI, SM, K to end. 2 gusset sts inc.

Rnds 2-4: K to M, SM, K to next M, SM, K to end.

Work Rnds 1-4 a total of 8 (9) times, until you have 18 (20) sts between gusset markers, ending on Rnd 4.

Next Rnd: Work to first gusset marker, remove marker, place the next 18 (20) thumb sts on waste yarn; CO 4 sts using the backward loop cast-on method, remove second gusset marker, K to end. 50 (66) sts

Work even until 8.25 (8.75)" from bottom edge of cuff, or to 1 (1.5)" less than desired length.

Top Decreases

Set Up Rnd: K25 (33) sts, PM for side, K to end.

Rnd 1: *K1, SSK, K to 3 sts before M, K2tog, K1; rep from *. 4 sts dec.

Rnd 2: Knit.

Work Rnds 1-2 4 (5) times, then Rnd 1 4 (7) times more. 18 sts remain.

Graft sts together using Kitchener Stitch.

Thumb

Starting at the right edge of the gap, with RS facing, pick up (pick up only, do not pick up and knit) 3 sts, PM for beginning of round marker, PU 3 sts, place remaining thumb sts onto needles. 6 sts picked up. 24 (26) sts.

Next Rnd: K1, K2tog, K to last 3 sts, SSK, K to end.

Next Rnd (Size small only): K2tog, K to last 2 sts, SSK, 20 (24) sts.

All Sizes: Knit until thumb is .25" less than desired length.

Decrease Rnd 1: (K2, K2tog) to end. 15 (18) sts.

Decrease Rnd 2: (K1, K2tog) to end. 10 (12) sts.

Decrease Rnd 3: (K2tog) to end. Break yarn and thread through remaining 5 (6) sts, pulling tightly to close hole.

Finishing

Weave in ends, wash and block to measurements.

Duplicate Stitching

Using Duplicate Stitch chart as a guide, work duplicate stitch.

Large Cuff Chart

Small Cuff Chart

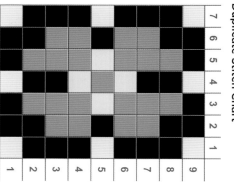

Duplicate Stitch Chart

Legend

knit
knit stitch

☐ knit

▨ MC

▨ C1

▨ C2

■ C3

COUNTING SHEEP CLOCK

by Rosalyn Jung

FINISHED MEASUREMENTS

11.75x11.75" (10.75x13.75").

YARN

Knit Picks Wool of the Andes Worsted (100% Peruvian Highland Wool; 110 yards/50g): MC Peapod 25983, C1 Coal 23420, 1 ball each.

Knit Picks Reverie (80% Baby Alpaca, 20% Acrylic; 137 yards/50g): C2 Natural 26113, 1 ball.

Eight 2' lengths of yarn from stash for flowers. Sample used Knit Picks Palette (100% Peruvian Highland Wool; 231 yards/50g): Canary 25531, Blush 23718, Cosmopolitan 24568, Wonderland Heather 26044, Mai Tai Heather 24555, Sky 23724, Cream 23730, Serrano 24553.

NEEDLES

US 7 (4.5mm) 24" circular needles, or size to obtain gauge

US 6 (4mm) 24" circular needles or 1 size smaller than needles to obtain gauge

NOTIONS

Scrap Yarn and Size J or I Crochet Hook for Provisional CO

Yarn Needle

12 Removable Stitch Markers

Pen Style 3-Needle Felting Tool and Mat

Clock Mechanism Kit for 3/8" (1 cm) thick surfaces (See Notes)

Shadow Box Picture Frame, 12x12" square or 11x14" rectangle (See Notes)

Fabric Glue and Foam Tip Brush or Wood Craft Stick

Drill and 5/16" Drill Bit (See Notes)

Protractor

GAUGE

18 sts and 24 rows = 4" in St st, blocked.

Both stitch and row gauges are necessary for accurate time.

For pattern support, contact KnitSewPretty@gmail.com

Counting Sheep Clock

Notes:

The Counting Sheep Clock is a picture of sheep and flowers in the meadow. They happen to appear in all the right places to help us tell time. Mark their positions in the grassy meadow as you knit. Duplicate stitch their heads and legs, needle felt their bodies and embroider the flowers. Add a thin black border to corral them.

The best frames are those with a recessed back that will wholly or partially accommodate the clock mechanism box. Other types of frames may be appropriate, including the T-shirt frames which usually have extra rear space. A no-drill option is to use artist's stretch canvas reinforced with a compact disc (a "CD") glued to the center back. See-through "floating" frames are not appropriate.

The clock mechanism should be designated for 3/8" thick clock faces. This shaft height will allow the hands to operate smoothly above the knitted fabric. The longest hand must be no longer than 3" (7.5 cm).

The sheep in the sample were needle felted onto the background. The pen style needle-felting tool with 3 needles allows for more precision felting. Alternatively, sheep may be worked in duplicate stitch as shown in Chart C.

The pattern is worked from the bottom up. Place removable markers on the stitches designated for sheep and flower placement. Instructions are given for 11.75" square clock, followed by instructions for 10.75x13.75" rectangular clock in parentheses.

Use MC to swatch for gauge. Keep the swatch in case you need to unravel it for the project. Clock face will require about 82 yards of MC.

Stockinette Stitch Pattern (worked flat)

Row 1 (RS): K across.

Row 2 (WS): P across.

Repeat Rows 1 and 2 for pattern.

Instructional Videos

Crochet Provisional CO: http://tutorials.knitpicks.com/
wptutorials/crocheted-provisional-cast-on/

Duplicate Stitch: http://tutorials.knitpicks.com/wptutorials/
embroidery-how-to-do-the-duplicate-stitch/

French Knots: http://tutorials.knitpicks.com/wptutorials/basic-
embroidery-tutorial/

DIRECTIONS

Preparation

Remove glass pane from the picture frame. Remove the kickstand if there is one. With the backing in place, trace an outline of the inner border from the front. Determine the exact center by drawing intersecting lines from corner to corner and from half way up and half way across to the opposite sides. Drill a 5/16" hole at the exact center. Test the size of the hole by inserting the clock shaft.

Background Meadow

With MC and larger needles, CO 53 (61) sts using the crochet provisional CO method. Purl 1 row. Begin Chart A or Chart B at RS Row 1. Place markers as shown in the charts. Or follow written instructions in lieu of charts as follows. Markers are to encircle the st, not to be placed between sts.

All Sizes: Beginning with a WS row, work 9 rows in St st.

Size 11.75x11.75" ONLY

Next Row (RS): K17, PM on last st, K to end.

P 1 WS row.

Next Row: K27, PM on last st, K20, PM on last st, K to end.

Work 8 rows in St st.

Next Row (WS): P10, PM on last st, P34, PM on last st, P to end.

Work 13 rows in St st.

Next Row (WS): P8, PM on last st, P19, PM on last st, P19, PM on last st, P to end.

Work 12 rows in St st.

Next Row (RS): K10, PM on last st, K34, PM on last st, K to end.

Work 9 rows in St st.

Next Row: K17, PM on last st, K20, PM on last st, K to end.

Work 12 rows in St st.

Next Row: K27, PM on last st, K to end.

Proceed to All Sizes, below.

Size 10.75x13.75" ONLY

Next Row (RS): K31, PM on last st, K to end.

Next Row (WS): P22, PM on last st, P18, PM on last st, P to end.

Work 7 rows in St st.

Next Row (WS): P14, PM on last st, P34, PM on last st, P to end.

Work 12 rows in St st.

Next Row (RS): K10, PM on last st, K21, PM on last st, K21, PM on last st, K to end.

Work 12 rows in St st.

Next Row (WS): P14, PM on last st, P34, PM on last st, P to end.

Work 7 rows in St st.

Next Row (WS): P31, PM on last st, P18, PM on last st, P to end.

Next Row: P31, PM on last st, P to end.

K 1 row.

All Sizes: Work 8 rows in St st. Leave live sts on circular needle after completing the meadow; do not bind off.

Border

Unravel the provisional CO and place live sts on the smaller circular needle. With C1 and RS facing, working from right to left, K the live sts from the provisional CO, KFB in the last st. PU and K 3 sts for every 4 rows up the right side edge. KFB in the last st. PU and K 3 sts for every 4 rows on the top edge. K to the last st, KFB. PU and K 3 sts for every 4 rows down the left side edge. KFB into the first st of the last round. Continuing in the round, bind off purlwise. Connect the round to bridge the gap.

Sheep

Heads and Legs

Thread a 2' length of C1 onto a yarn needle. Follow Chart C to duplicate stitch the heads and legs. The marker for the sheep is the point of the nose. Place the sheep at the 12, 3, 6, and 9 positions of the clock.

Sheep Bodies

With C2, needle felt a 2" oval of "fluff" at each sheep position. Felt in a curlicue fashion, avoiding the head and legs but getting close enough to prevent any background green from peeking through. Alternatively, duplicate stitch the bodies as shown in Chart C with a double strand of C2.

Flowers

Using short lengths of yarn from stash in your choice of colors, embroider five Lazy Daisy Flower petals, each 0.5" long, at each marker between the sheep. Remove the markers and embroider French knots at flower centers. Also work six petals, each 0.75" long, around (not through) the clock center stitch to form a flower under the clock hands.

How to work Lazy Daisy Flowers: Insert needle from the underside to the surface through the marked stitch. Lay a loop on the surface with the working yarn. Insert needle back down the same place it came out of, then insert needle back up to the surface 0.5" away and inside the loop of yarn. Tighten the loop to form a petal. Anchor the petal by inserting the needle just outside the loop to the underside. Start each petal from the flower center (the marked stitch).

Finishing

Weave in ends gently for 2 sts only and trim tails to 0.5" long. Wet or steam block to finished measurements. Let dry completely. Test the size inside the picture frame.

Working from top to bottom, across one quarter of the surface area at a time, spread an even layer of fabric glue within the marked border of the frame backing. Carefully lay the fabric onto the glue, making sure the sheep and flowers are evenly spaced apart and the St st background is not distorted. Check sheep and flower placement with a protractor. Each sheep should be 90° apart from each other and each flower/sheep should be 30° apart in a 360° circle.

Make sure the minute hand will not touch the sheep. Put a little extra glue at the corners if necessary to hold them down.

When the clock face is dry, assemble the clock mechanism as directed on the package. Place the rubber cushion over the shaft. Insert the clock shank through the drilled hole and the knit fabric, clipping one strand of knitting if necessary. Add the remaining nuts, hands and screws in the order directed. Insert a battery and hang the clock on the wall.

Chart C

	7	6	5	4	3	2	1	
								13
								12
	■	■	■	■				11
	■	■	■	■	■	■		10
	■	■	■	■	■			9
	■	■	■	■				8
	■	■	■	■				7
	■	■	■	■	■	■		6
				■	■	■		5
								4
	■	■	■					3
	■	■	■					2
	■	■	■					1

Chart A: Marker placement chart for 12" square clock

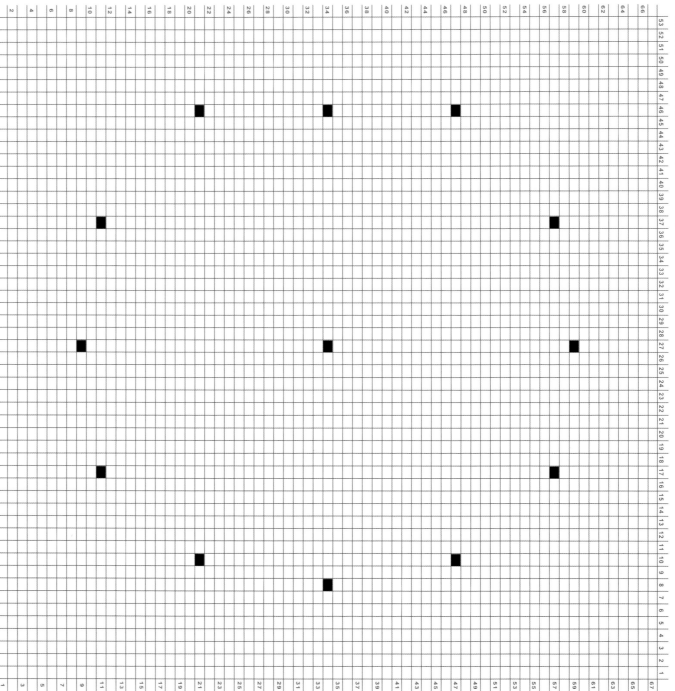

Chart B: Marker placement for 11x14" rectangular clock

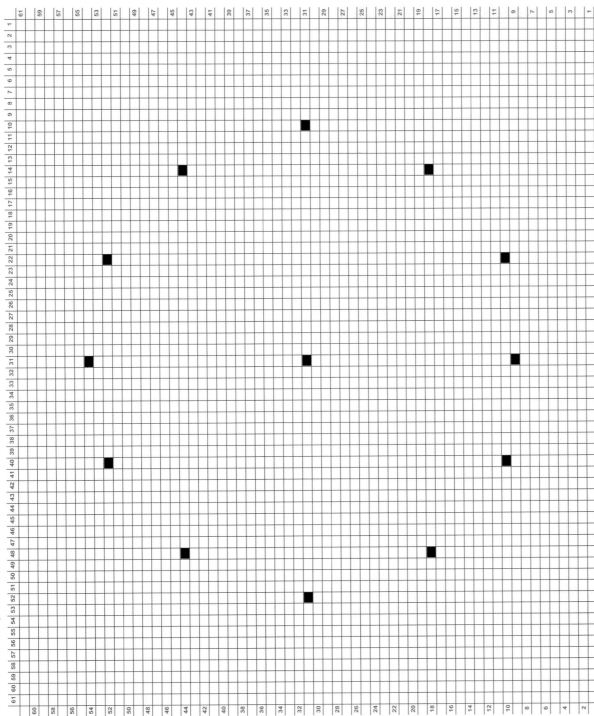

MIRROR MIRROR MOEBIUS

by Kath Andrews

FINISHED MEASUREMENTS

7.25" wide x 50.5" circumference

YARN

Knit Picks Lindy Chain (70% Linen, 30% Pima Cotton; 180 yards/50g): Honey 26458, 2 balls.

NEEDLES

US 8 (5mm) 40" circular needle, or size to obtain gauge

NOTIONS

Yarn Needle
Stitch Marker

GAUGE

14 sts and 18 rnds = 4" over Lace Pattern in the round, blocked. (Gauge for this project is not crucial)

Mirror Mirror Moebius

Notes:

Video instructions for Cat Bordhi's Moebius Cast On can be found at https://www.youtube.com/watch?v=LVnTda7F2V4.

Lace Stitch Pattern (In the round over multiple of 3 sts)

Rnd 1: (P1, YO, P2tog) to end.

Rnd 2: (P1, K2tog, YO) to end.

Rnd 3: Repeat Rnd 1.

Rnd 4: Repeat Rnd 2.

Reverse Lace Stitch Pattern (In the round over multiple of 3 sts)

Rnd 1: (K1, YO, K2tog) to end.

Rnd 2: (K1, P2tog, YO) to end.

Rnd 3: Repeat Rnd 1.

Rnd 4: Repeat Rnd 2.

DIRECTIONS

Cast on 180 sts using Cat Bordhi's Moebius Cast On, placing stitch marker at end of round. This will give 360 sts to work per round.

Central Garter Stitch Band

Rnd 1: Knit.

Rnd 2: Purl.

Rnd 3: Knit.

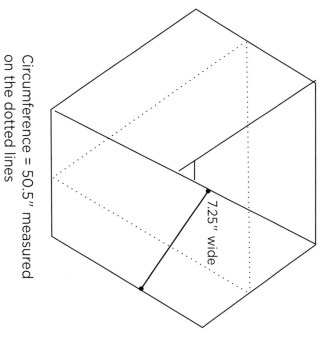

7.25" wide

Circumference = 50.5" measured on the dotted lines

Lace Pattern Band

Rnds 4-7: Work Rnds 1-4 of Lace Stitch Pattern.

Garter Stitch Band

Rnds 8, 10, 12 & 14: Purl.

Rnds 9, 11 & 13: Knit.

Reverse Lace Pattern Band

Rnds 15-18: Works Rnds 1-4 of Reverse Lace Stitch Pattern.

Garter Stitch Band

Rnds 19, 21, 23 & 25: Knit.

Rnds 20, 22 & 24: Purl.

Rnds 26-35: Rep Rnds 4-13.

Rnd 36: Bind off P-wise.

Finishing

Weave in ends, wash and block to diagram.

TRANSITIONS BOOT CUFFS

by Jenny Williams

FINISHED MEASUREMENTS

12" diameter x 5.5" high

YARN

Knit Picks Palette (100% Peruvian
Highland Wool; 231 yards/50g): C1
Asphalt 24243, C2 Ash 23731, C3
Cosmopolitan 24568, C4 Silver 24586, C5
Cream 23730; 1 ball each

NEEDLES

US 2 (3mm) DPNs or circular needles, or
size to obtain gauge
US 1 (2.25mm) DPNs or circular needles,
or one size smaller than needles to obtain
gauge

NOTIONS

Yarn Needle
Stitch Markers

GAUGE

37 sts and 39 rows = 4" using larger
needles in stranded St st in the rnd,
blocked.

For pattern support, contact jennyw@tcworks.net

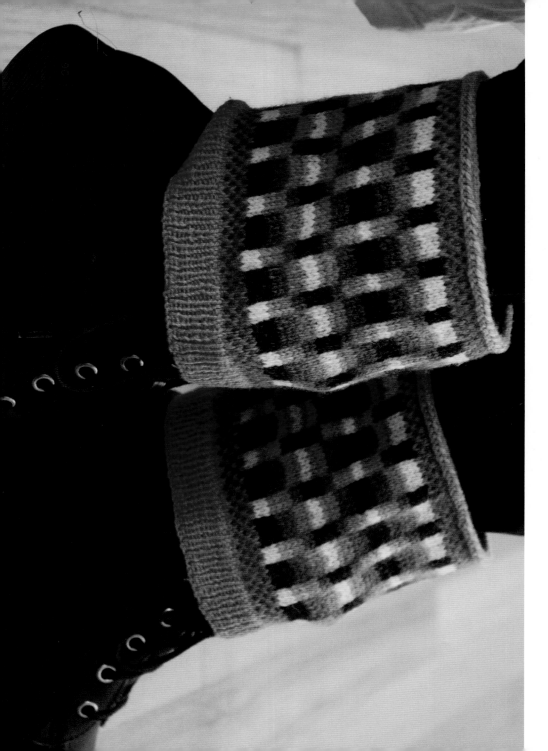

Transitions Boot Cuffs

Notes:

These boot cuffs are worked from the bottom up, in the round, using the traditional Fair Isle 2 strand method. The Transitions Chart is meant to be worked with 5 colors, arranged from light to dark. It may help to lay the skeins side by side and squint at them, in order to see the different values. Another option is to photograph the skeins and convert the photo to black and white using your photo editor.

The chart rows are followed from right to left, knitting all stitches.

Knitted Cast On

Begin with a slip knot on the left needle. Knit one st into the slip knot, sliding the knit stitch back onto the left needle. *K1 into the knit st, sliding st back onto left needle. Repeat from * for the number of sts required.

DIRECTIONS

Using the Knitted Cast On method, the smaller circular needles and C3, loosely cast on 104 sts. PM to mark beginning of the rnd. Join to begin working in the rnd, taking care not to twist the sts.

Ribbing

Rib Rnd: *K1, P1, rep from * to end of rnd. Work Rib Rnd for 1".

Increase Rnd: *K12, KFB, rep from * to end of rnd. 8 sts inc. 112 sts total.

Body

Change to larger needles. Begin working Transitions Chart. *work Row 1 sts 1-8, PM, rep from * 12 more times across rnd. Continue working Transitions Chart through Row 40, removing markers on last rnd. Do not break C3 or C4.

Note: If a color spans more than 3 sts, twist the two yarns on the WS to carry the second color. This is called a "float". To avoid grooves on the RS, alternate the float twists from just before the third st to just before the fourth st, every other row.

Latvian Braid

First Rnd: Bring both working yarns to the front. *P1 in C4, cross strand of C3 over strand just worked, P1 in C3, cross C4 over strand just worked. Repeat from * to end of rnd.

Next Rnd: Work as for previous rnd, but cross next strand UNDER strand just worked.

Bind Off

Using C3, *BO 6 sts K-wise, K2tog TBL. Pass second st on right needle over K2tog st. Repeat from * to end of rnd.

Finishing

Weave in ends. Use rolled up hand towel and wet block to desired size.

Transitions Chart

Legend

☐	knit
	knit stitch
■	C1
▨	C2
▨	C3
▨	C4
☐	C5

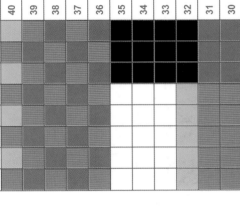
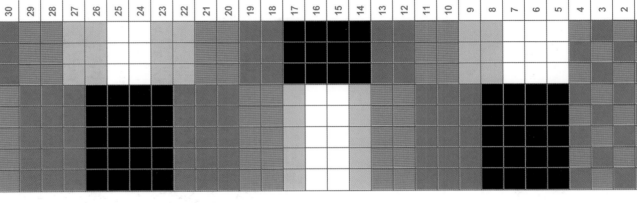

WOODMERE MITTS

by Triona Murphy

FINISHED MEASUREMENTS

7.5" palm circumference, 8.5" long from bottom of cuff to top

YARN

Knit Picks Wool of the Andes Sport (100% Peruvian Highland Wool; 137 yards/50g):

Colorwork Mitts: MC Marina 25290, C1 Dove Heather 25656, 1 ball each.

Solid Mitts: Blossom Heather 25306, 2 balls.

NEEDLES

US 4 (3.5mm) DPNs or two 24" circular needles for two circulars technique, or one 32" or longer circular needle for Magic Loop technique, or size to obtain gauge.

US 3 (3.25mm) DPNs or two 24" circular needles for two circulars technique, or one 32" or longer circular needle for Magic Loop technique, or one size smaller than gauge needle.

NOTIONS

Yarn Needle
Stitch Marker
Scrap Yarn

GAUGE

Colorwork Mitts: 29 sts and 30 rnds = 4" in stranded St st in the round on larger needles, blocked.

Plain Mitts: 24 sts and 30 rnds = 4" in St st in the round on larger needles, blocked.

For pattern support, contact triona@trionadesigns.com

Woodmere Mitts

Notes:
Complete directions for the two styles of Mitts, Colorwork and Plain, are given separately.

1x1 Rib
All Rnds: *K1, P1; rep from * to end.

COLORWORK VERSION

Notes: These playful two-color mitts, sized to fit an average woman's hand, feature a totally different stranded colorwork pattern on the palm and the back of the hand, so there's no chance to get bored. A striped thumb gusset adds comfort and style.

When working MIR and MIL increases for thumb, you will see two strands of yarn between sts. Pick up only the strand in the color indicated for that increase on the Thumb Chart. The chart rows are all followed from right to left.

DIRECTIONS
Right Mitt
Cuff

With MC, CO 54 sts on smaller needles. Join for working in the round, being careful not to twist, PM to indicate the beginning of the rnd and begin 1x1 Rib.

Work 1x1 Rib until work measures 1.25" from CO edge.

Begin Main Pattern
Switch to larger needles and work Rnd 1 of Chart A over first 27 sts, then Rnd 1 of Chart B over next 27 sts.

Continue in this manner, working the next rnd of Chart A, then the next rnd of Chart B, until one full repeat (18 rnds) of Chart A has been worked (three full repeats of Chart B).

Thumb Gusset (See pattern notes for instructions on how to work increases in the correct color)
Setup Rnd: Work 27 sts of Chart A, work first 4 sts of Chart B, PM, work Rnd 1 of Thumb Chart (Note: the center st of this chart is also the 5th st of Chart B), PM, work remainder of Chart B over last 22 sts. 2 gusset sts inc.

Next Rnd: Work one rnd even in pattern as set without increases. Note: the center st of thumb should always be worked in the MC as shown on Thumb Chart. Skip the 5th st when working Chart B until thumb gusset is complete.
Thumb Increase Rnd: Work in pattern as set, including the next set of increases as indicated on Thumb Chart. 2 sts inc.

Repeat last two rnds 6 more times. 17 sts between thumb markers, 70 sts total.

Next Rnd: Work in pattern as set to first thumb marker, remove marker, slip next 17 sts to scrap yarn. Using MC, CO 1 st over the gap using the backwards loop method, remove second marker, work to end of rnd in pattern. 54 sts.

Continue in pattern as set (incorporating CO st back into Chart B) until two full repeats (36 rnds) of Chart A have been worked from beginning of colorwork, then work the first 9 rnds of Chart A again. Cut C1. Piece should measure approximately 7.25" from CO edge.

Switch to smaller needles and knit 1 rnd even with MC.

Work 1x1 Rib with MC for 1.25". BO all sts in pattern.

Finish Thumb
Return 17 held thumb sts to larger needles. Rejoin MC and C1 to right edge.

Next Rnd: *K1 with MC, K1 with C1; rep from * to last st, K1 with MC. PU and K 1 st C1, 1 st MC, 1 st C1, 1 st MC, 1 st C1 in the gap. 22 sts on the needles.

Knit in pattern as set (alternating MC and C1) for 3 rnds. Cut C1.

Switch to smaller needles and knit 1 rnd even with MC.

Work 1x1 Rib with MC for 4 rnds.

BO all sts in pattern.

Left Mitt
Work as for Right Mitt to Thumb Gusset.

Thumb Gusset
Setup Rnd: Work 27 sts of Chart A, work Chart B to last 5 sts of rnd, PM, work Rnd 1 of Thumb Chart (Note: the center st of this chart is also the 5th st from the end of Chart B), PM, work remainder of Chart B over last 4 sts. 2 gusset sts inc.

Work remainder of Thumb Gusset, Mitt, and Thumb Finishing as for Right Mitt.

Finishing (both mitts)
Weave in ends, wash and block.

SOLID VERSION
DIRECTIONS
Right Mitt
Cuff

CO 46 sts on smaller needles. Join for working in the round, being careful not to twist, PM to indicate the beginning of the rnd and begin 1x1 Rib.

Work 1x1 Rib until work measures 1.25" from CO edge.

Switch to larger needles. Knit 18 rnds.

Thumb Gusset
Setup Rnd: K 25 sts, PM, MIR, K1, MIL, PM, K to end. 2 gusset sts inc.

Next Rnd: Knit one rnd even without increases.
Thumb Increase Rnd: K to first M, SM, MIR, K to second M, MIL, SM, K to end. 2 sts inc.

Repeat last two rnds 5 more times. 15 sts between thumb markers, 60 sts total.

Next Rnd: K to first thumb marker, remove marker, slip next 15 sts to scrap yarn, CO 1 st over the gap using the backwards loop method, remove second marker, work to end of rnd in pattern. 46 sts.

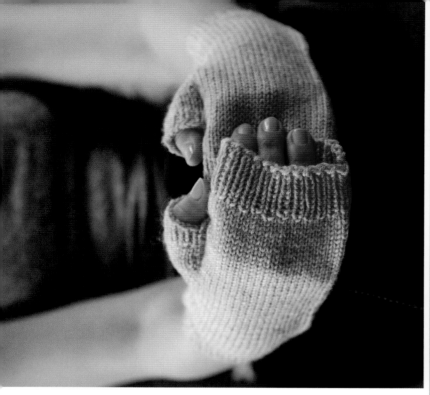

Knit even until piece measures 7.25" from CO edge.

Switch to smaller needles. Work 1x1 Rib as for Cuff for 1.25". BO all sts in pattern.

Finish Thumb

Return 15 held thumb sts to larger needles. Rejoin yarn to right edge.

Next Rnd: K to last st, PU and K 3 sts in the gap. 18 sts on the needles.

Knit for 4 rnds.

Switch to smaller needles. Work 1x1 Rib for 4 rnds.

BO all sts in pattern.

Left Mitt

Work as for Right Mitt to Thumb Gusset.

Thumb Gusset

Setup Rnd: K to last 3 sts of rnd, PM, M1R, K1, M1L, PM, K2 to end. 2 gusset sts inc.

Work remainder of Thumb Gusset, Mitt, and Thumb Finishing as for Right Mitt.

Finishing (both mitts)

Weave in ends, wash and block.

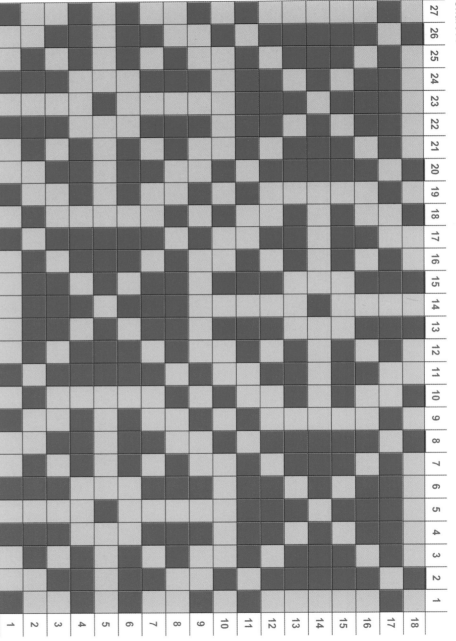

Legend

MC

C1

No Stitch
Placeholder - no
stitch made

make one right
Lift the horizontal thread
between your needles with
your left needle tip from
back to front. Knit this
newly lifted stitch.

make one left
Lift the horizontal thread
between your needles
with your left needle tip
from front to back. Knit
this newly lifted stitch
through the back loop.

Chart B

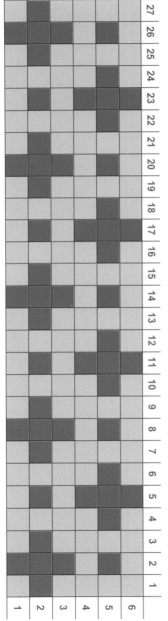

Thumb Chart

	15	14	13	12	11	10	9	8	7	6	5	4	3	2	1
1	MR														
2			MR												
3					MR										
4						MR									
5							MR								
6									MR						
7											MR				
8													MR		
9															
10													ML		
11											ML				
12									ML						
13							ML								
14					ML										
15			ML												
16		ML													
17	ML														

TREACLE MOUNTAIN HAT

by Lynnette Hulse

FINISHED MEASUREMENTS

To fit newborn (baby, toddler, child, adult, large adult) 12 (14, 16, 18, 20, 22)" circumference. Hat is meant to be worn with 2" of ease.

YARN

Knit Picks Wool of the Andes Superwash (100% Superwash Wool; 110 yards/50g):

2-color version: MC White 26326, 2 balls; C1 Cobblestone Heather 26304, 1 ball.

Solid version: Haze Heather 26320, 3 balls.

NEEDLES

US 7 (4.5mm) DPNs or circular needles, or size to obtain gauge

NOTIONS

Yarn Needle
Stitch Marker
PomPom Maker

GAUGE

23 sts and 28 rows = 4" over rib pattern, blocked

26 sts and 14 rows = 4" over lace & bobble pattern, blocked (Gauge for this project is approximate)

Treacle Mountain Hat

Notes:

This hat features a tubular cast on that changes color before the five-row process is complete. The lace and bobble pattern is supplied both charted and written. Chart rows are all followed from right to left.

MB (Make Bobble): Knit front, back and then front again in same st. Turn work and P3 sts, turn and K3, turn and P3. Turn and K all 3 sts together.

KFSB: Knit front leg of st, slip back leg, 1 st inc.

P2SSO: Pass two slipped sts over. 2 sts dec.

Treacle Mountain Motif (in the round over multiples of 14 sts)

Round 1: *YO, K1, P4, SL2, K1, P2SSO, P4, K1, YO, K1; rep from * to end of rnd.

Round 2: *YO, K1, MB, P3, SL2, K1, P2SSO, P3, MB, K1, YO, K1; rep from * to end of rnd.

Round 3: *YO, K3, P2, SL2, K1, P2SSO, P2, K3, YO, K1; rep from * to end of rnd.

Round 4: *YO, K3, MB, P1, SL2, K1, P2SSO, P1, MB, K3, YO, K1; rep from * to end of rnd.

Round 5: *YO, K5, SL2, K1, P2SSO, K5, YO, K1; rep from * to end of rnd.

Round 6: *YO, K4, SSK, MB, K2TOG, K4, YO, K1; rep from * to end of rnd.

Repeat Rounds 1-6 for pattern.

Tubular Cast On

Step 1: Leaving a tail approximately three times the circumference of size working, make a loop and place it on the right needle and secure the loop with your right index finger. Holding the needle in the right hand and both working yarn and tail in the left, insert the left thumb and index finger down in between the two strands, then turn your fingers back up, spreading them apart at the same time. The tail should now be wrapped around the thumb and the working yarn wrapped around your index finger.

Step 2: Bring the needle over the thumb strand, down under it, and up between the two strands.

Step 3: Bring the needle over the finger strand and back down beneath it.

Step 4: Bring the needle under the thumb strand and up, creating a knit stitch.

Step 5: Bring the needle over, behind, and under the index finger strand, and then forward and up between the two strands.

Step 6: Bring the needle over the thumb strand, down and back under both strands, bring the needle up to create a purl stitch on the needle.

Repeat steps 2-6 until you have the required number of sts, not counting the original loop. Turn, wrap the tail counterclockwise around the working strand to secure the last stitch.

DIRECTIONS
Set Up Rows

Working flat and using C1, CO 70 (82, 92, 102, 112, 122) sts in Tubular Cast On to prepare for 1x1 rib.

Row 1: *K1 TBL, SL1 WYIF; rep from * to end, dropping the first set up loop when you come to it.

Row 2: *K1, SL1 WYIF; rep from * to end.

Change to MC.

Rows 3-4: Repeat Row 2.

Brim

Step 1: SL1, *P1, K1; rep from * to end, ending with a P1. Repeat Step 1 12 (12, 16, 16, 16, 20) times.

Step 2: Continue in 1x1 rib for 6 (8, 8, 10, 10) rounds.

Join to work in the round, PM to denote beginning of round, SM as you come to it.

Step 3a, For sizes 14 (16, 18, 22)" ONLY:

14": *K40, KFB* to end. 84 sts.

16": *K14, KFB* 6 times, K2. 98 sts.

18": *K9, KFB* 10 times, K2. 112 sts.

22": *K29, KFB* 4 times, K2. 126 sts.

Step 3b. For all sizes EXCEPT 18": *K4 (5, 6, -, 7, 8), KFSB; rep from * to end. 84 (98, 112, 112, 126, 140) sts.

Cap

Step 1: Repeat Treacle Mountain Motif 1 (1, 2, 3, 3, 3) times

Change to C1.

Step 2: *YO, K5, SL2, K1, P2SSO, K5, YO, K1; rep from * to end.

Step 3: Work Treacle Mountain Motif 1 (1, 1, 1, 1, 2) times.

Step 4: *YO, K2, SSK, K1, SL2, K1, P2SSO, K1, K2TOG, K2, YO, K1; rep from * to end. 72 (84, 96, 96, 108, 120) sts.

Step 5: *YO, K2, SSK, SL2, K1, P2SSO, K2TOG, K2, YO, K1; rep from * to end. 60 (70, 80, 80, 90, 100) sts.

Step 6: *YO, K1, SSK, SL2, K1, P2SSO, K2TOG, K1, YO, K1; rep from * to end. 48 (56, 64, 64, 72, 80) sts.

Step 7: *K2, SL2, K1, P2SSO, K3; rep from * to end. 36 (42, 48, 48, 54, 60) sts.

Step 8: *SSK, K1, K2TOG, K1; rep from * to end. 24 (28, 32, 32, 36, 40) sts.

Step 9: *SL2, K1, P2SSO, K1; rep from * to end. 12 (14, 16, 16, 18, 20) sts.

Step 10:

12 and 20" ONLY: *SL2, K1, P2SSO; rep from * to end. 4 (6) sts.

14" ONLY: K2TOG to end. 7 sts.

16 and 18" ONLY: *SL2, K1, P2SSO, K1; rep from * to end. 8 sts.

22" ONLY: *K3TOG, K2TOG; rep from * to end. 8 sts.

Finishing

Break yarn, remove marker, and thread tail through embroidery needle. Slip yarn needle through each of the remaining sts, take sts off needles, and pull tail tight to close. Weave in all ends. Block to size, if blocking rib only block vertically. With C1, make a 1.75 (2.5, 2.5, 3.75, 3.75, 3.75)" pompom, leaving a long tail; use tail to attach pompom to center top of hat.

Treacle Mountain Chart

	6	5	4	3	2	1
14						
13	O	O	O	O	O	O
12						
11					◇	•
10					•	•
9			◇	•	•	•
8	\			•	•	•
7	◇	⋀	⋀	⋀	⋀	⋀
6	/		•	•	•	•
5			◇	•	•	•
4					•	•
3					◇	•
2						
1	O	O	O	O	O	O

Legend

- **yo** — yarn over (O)
- **knit** — knit stitch (empty square)
- **purl** — purl stitch (•)
- **k2tog** — knit two stitches together as one stitch (/)
- **sl2 k1 psso** — sl2 sts, k1 st, pass two slipped sts over. (⋀)
- **bobble** — knit front, back and then front again in same st. Turn work and P3 sts, turn and K3, turn and P3. Turn and K all 3 sts together. (◇)
- **ssk** — slip one stitch as if to knit, Slip another stitch as if to knit. Insert left-hand needle into front of these 2 stitches and knit them together (\)

CHEVRON WINE COZY

by Ursula Almeida

FINISHED MEASUREMENTS

4.5x11.5" high, measured flat

YARN

Knit Picks Wool of the Andes Worsted (100% Peruvian Highland Wool; 110 yards/50g): MC White 24065, C1 Dove Heather 24077, C2 Blossom Heather 25067, 1 ball each.

NEEDLES

US 6 (4mm) DPNs or two 24" circular needles for two circulars technique, or one 32" or longer circular needle for Magic Loop technique plus 2 DPN's for I-Cord, or size to obtain gauge

NOTIONS

Yarn Needle
Stitch Markers
Scrap Yarn
Size H Crochet Hook for Provisional CO

GAUGE

21 sts and 25 rows = 4" in stranded St st in the round, blocked.

Chevron Wine Cozy

Notes:

This cozy starts with a provisional cast on, then stranded colorwork is worked from a chart in the round for the body followed by ribbing worked in the main color for the neck. Provisional stitches are then picked up, working decreases to close up the bottom of the cozy. Finish off with pompoms attached to an I-cord tie.

The chart is worked in the round, follow each chart row from right to left.

I-Cord

Using a DPN, CO 3 sts. *Knit a row. Slide row to other end of needle without turning work. Pull yarn firmly and repeat from * creating a tube.

DIRECTIONS

Body of Cozy

With MC, provisionally CO 48 sts. Join in the round and knit 1 round in MC. Join C1 and work Rows 1-22 of Chart 2 times, repeating motif 4 times across the round. Work rows 45-49 of Chart 1 time, repeating 4 times across the round, taking care to carry C1 loosely. Before cutting C1 and weaving in the end, slip bottle into cozy to ensure fit. Next work Neck Ribbing.

Neck Ribbing

Round 1: (K1, P1) to end.

Rounds 2-10: Repeat Rnd 1.

Round 11 (eyelet round): *K1, YO, (P1, K1) 2 times, P1; repeat from * 8 times.

Round 12: *K1, P2tog, (K1, P1) 2 times; repeat from * 8 times.

Rounds 13-19: Repeat Rnd 1.

Bind off with preferred stretchy bind off such as Sewn Kitchener Bind Off.

Bottom of Cozy

Put provisionally CO stitches on needles. PM at beginning of round.

Round 1: With MC, K to end.

Round 2: (SSK, K8, K2tog) 4 times. 40 sts.

Round 3: Knit.

Round 4: (SSK, K6, K2tog) 4 times. 32 sts.

Round 5: (SSK, K4, K2tog) 4 times. 24 sts.

Round 6: (SSK, K2, K2tog) 4 times. 16 sts.

Round 7: (SSK, K2tog) 4 times. 8 sts.

Round 8: (SSK, K2tog) 2 times. 4 sts.

Cut yarn, weave through live stitches, and secure.

Finishing

Weave in ends, wash and block over bottle, making sure to remove as much water from the cozy as possible so as not to wet the label on the wine bottle while also taking care not to felt the wool. Alternately, steam block over bottle and allow to dry.

Knit a 9" length of 3 st I-cord in MC. Thread through eyelet round. Create two 1.5" pompoms in C2, then attach to both ends of I-cord.

Chevron Chart

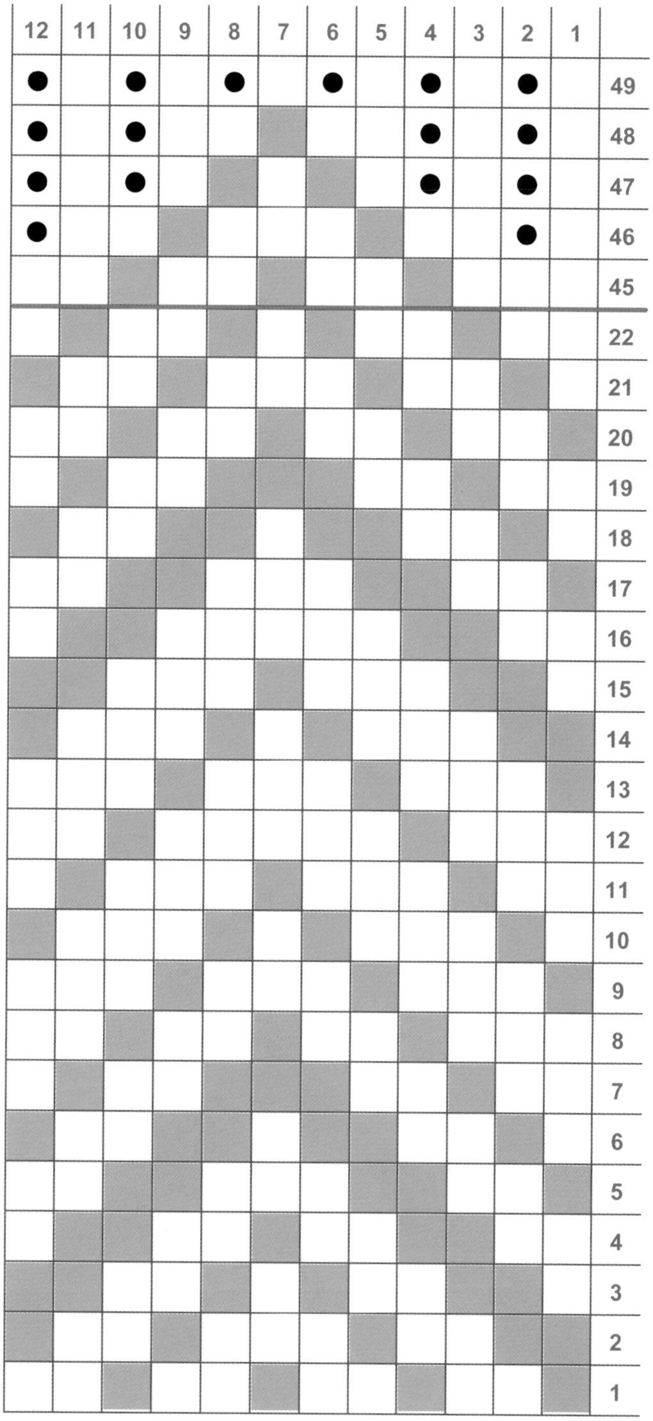

Legend

- **knit** knit stitch
- **purl** purl stitch
- C1
- MC
- repeat

FLUTTER

by Kimberly Voisin

FINISHED MEASUREMENTS

7" back depth, 58.5" along bottom edge

YARN

Knit Picks Capretta (80% Fine Merino Wool, 10% Cashmere, 10% Nylon; 230 yards/50g):

Solid Color Shawl: MC Platinum 25595; 2 balls

Multi-Color Shawl: MC Cream 25600, C1 Harbor 25598, C2 Sagebrush 26563; 1 ball each

NEEDLES

US 5 (3.75mm) 2 sets of 40" circular needles, or size to obtain gauge.

NOTIONS

Yarn Needle

Stitch Markers

Spare Circular Needle, Needle Cord, or Stitch Holders

GAUGE

22 sts and 40 rows = 4" over garter stitch, blocked.

For pattern support, contact kimberly_voisin@hotmail.com

Flutter

Notes:

Flutter was created with stash busting in mind. The layered scallops make this the perfect project for using up extra bits of yarn or for justifying purchasing your favorite yarn in multiple colors.

The shawlette is constructed of layers of garter stitch scallops. Each color layer is constructed individually and the layers are assembled by knitting them together. Although this sounds complex, the technique of creating the layers is straightforward. The main body of the shawl is narrow and created with short rows, resulting in a curved shawl which is easy to wrap around the shoulders.

3-Needle Join

Work stitches of both layers together using the 3-needle joining technique as follows: With RS of layers facing up (top layer over the bottom layer) and the needles parallel, insert a third needle into the first stitch of each needle and work them together.

Knit into the front and back (KFB)

Knit into the front of the loop, like you normally would. Without removing the st from the needle, knit through the back loop of the st. 1 st inc.

DIRECTIONS

Pattern is written to reflect the multi-color version of the shawlette. If knitting a single color shawlette please disregard references to color switches and use MC throughout.

Scalloped Edge

Bottom Scallop (make 21)

With C1, CO 5 sts.

Row 1: Knit.

Row 2: Kfb, K to end.

Repeat Row 2 until there are 14 sts on the needle.

Place finished scallops on a stitch holder or spare circular needle.

Place all 21 completed scallops on one needle with the back of the work facing forward. The top row will look like a row of purls.

Row 1, Join Scallops: K across, being careful to close the gap between each scallop. 294 sts.

Row 2: Knit.

Repeat Row 2, 4 more times.

Set aside.

Middle Scallop (make 22)

Using C2, repeat Bottom Scallop directions.

Place all 22 completed scallops on one needle with the back of the work facing forward. The top row will look like a row of purls.

Row 1, Join Scallops: K across, being careful to close the gap between each scallop. 308 sts.

Row 2: Knit.

Repeat Row 2, two more times.

Top Scallop (make 23)

Using MC, repeat Bottom Scallop directions.

Place all 23 completed scallops on one needle with the back of the work facing forward. The top row will look like a row of purls.

Row 1, Join Scallops: K across, being careful to close the gap between each scallop. 322 sts.

Row 2: Knit.

Repeat Row 2, two more times.

Join Bottom and Middle Scallop Layers

Row 1: K the first 7 sts of the middle scallop layer. To join the layers, hold the needle with the middle scallops over the needle with the bottom scallops. Make sure that both scallop layers are facing wrong side up. Using the 3-Needle Join technique, K the two layers together. K the last of the middle scallop layer sts.

Rows 2 and 3: Knit

Repeat Row 2, two more times.

Join Bottom and Middle Scallop Layers to Top Scallop Layer

Row 1: K the first 7 sts of the top scallop layer. To join the layers, hold the needle with the bottom and middle scallops over the needle with the top scallops. Make sure that all scallop layers are facing wrong side up. Using the 3-Needle Join technique, K the two layers together. K the last of the top scallop layer sts.

Row 2: Knit.

Repeat Row 2, two more times.

Body of Shawl

Continue to work in MC.

Row 1: Knit 163 sts, turn.

Row 2: Knit 4 sts, turn.

Row 3: K to 1 st before the turning point, K2tog, K5, turn.

Row 4: K to 1 st before the turning point, K2tog, K5, turn.

Repeat Rows 3 and 4 until all of the sts have been worked. 269 sts.

BO loosely.

Finishing

Weave in ends, wash and block to Finished Measurements.

WEATHER MUG COZIES

by Emily Kintigh

FINISHED MEASUREMENTS

8.25" circumference, unfastened x 3.25" high, will fit cups approximately 11" around

YARN

Knit Picks Swish Worsted (100% Superwash Merino Wool; 110 yards/50g):

MC Wonderland Heather 26067, C1 Rouge 26071, C2 Honey 26066, C3 Marine Heather 24094, C4 Marble Heather 25153, C5 White 24662, 1 ball each.

NEEDLES

US 6 (4mm) straight or circular needles, or size to obtain gauge

NOTIONS

Yarn Needle

Removable Stitch Markers

Two .75" Buttons per Cozy

Size G Crochet hook

GAUGE

22 sts and 28 rows = 4" in St st, blocked.

For pattern support, contact auntieemsstudio@gmail.com

Weather Mug Cozies

Notes:

These mug cozies require very little yarn. One ball of the MC is enough to make a set of four cozies. Very small amounts are needed of all the other colors, making this project a great way to use up scrap yarn.

Make a set of four, pick your favorite, or even make a cozy that is sunny on one side and rainy on the other.

DIRECTIONS

Cozy

Loosely CO 45 sts.

Row 1 (WS): (K1, P1) to last st, K1.

Rows 2-4: Repeat Row 1.

Row 5: K1, P1, K1, P to last 3 sts, K1, P1, K1.

Row 6: K1, P1, K to last 2 sts, P1, K1.

Rows 7-21: Repeat Rows 5-6 seven more times, then Row 5 once more. After Row 7, place a removable stitch marker on 5th st from end of last row before continuing on. (To make a cozy with two designs, also place a marker on the 17th st from the beginning of the last row.)

Rows 22-25: Repeat Row 1.

BO all sts.

Loop (Make Two)

Using crochet hook, make a 4.5" long chain leaving long tails at beginning and end for attaching loops to the cozy.

Finishing

With the first stitch of the first row of the chart being the stitch marked with the removable stitch marker, use duplicate stitch to add the desired design. Work from the Rainbow Chart, Sunshine Chart, Rain Cloud Chart, or Snowflake Chart as needed. For the Sunshine Chart, use embroidery to form the rays coming out around the sun.

Sew loops to the top and bottom corner of one side of the cozy. Sew buttons to the top and bottom of the other side of the cozy.

Weave in ends, wash and block to measurements.

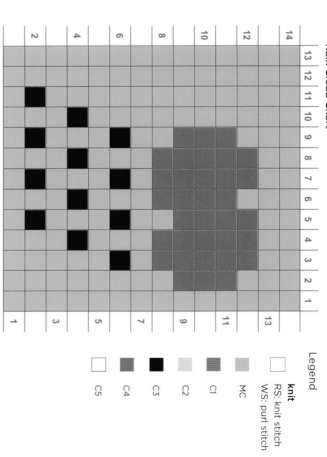

Rain Cloud Chart

Sunshine Chart

Legend

knit
RS: knit stitch
WS: purl stitch

MC

C1

C2

C3

C4

C5

Rainbow Chart

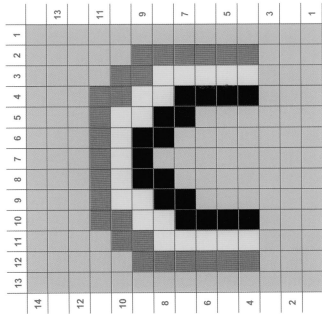

Snowflake Chart

KAPOWSKI LEG WARMERS

by Kimberly Golynskiy

FINISHED MEASUREMENTS

Kids one-size (Adult one-size): 10 (16)" long x 9 (11.5)" around, unblocked.

YARN

Knit Picks Stroll (75% Superwash Merino Wool, 25% Nylon; 231 yards/50g): MC White 26082, 2 balls; C1 Tranquil 26083, C2 Dandelion 25024, 1 ball each; Adult size only C3 Dogwood 25603, 1 ball.

NEEDLES

US 3 (3.25mm) DPNs or two 24" circular needles for two circulars technique, or one 32" or longer circular needle for Magic Loop technique, or size to obtain gauge

US 1 (2.25mm) DPNs or two 24" circular needles for two circulars technique, or one 32" or longer circular needle for Magic Loop technique, or 2 sizes smaller than needle to obtain gauge

NOTIONS

Yarn Needle

Stitch Markers

GAUGE

28 sts and 33 rnds = 4" in St st in the round on larger needle, unblocked.

Kapowski Leg Warmers

Notes:

These legwarmers are worked in the round from the bottom up with ribbed cuffs and charted colorwork chevrons and dots.

DIRECTIONS

Bottom Cuff

With MC CO 64 (80) sts, using the slip knot cast-on or your favorite stretchy cast-on, on smaller needles. Place marker and join in the round, being careful not to twist sts.

Round 1, Ribbing: (K1, P1) to end.
Repeat Round 1 15 (30) times.

Body

Switch to larger needles.

Round 1: Knit.

Repeat this round 5 (10) times.

Work Chevron Chart.

Work Dots Chart.

Break contrast color, continue with MC only.

Repeat Round One 15 (30) times.

Top Cuff

Switch to smaller needles.

Round 1 (Ribbing): (K1, P1) to end.
Repeat Round One 20 (40) times.

Kitchener Closing

Row 1: *K1, bring yarn forward, Sl 1 P-wise, return yarn to back; rep from * to end.

Row 2: *Sl 1 P-wise, bring yarn forward, P1, bring yarn to back; rep from * to end.

Using two sets of circular needles or 2 DPNs, separate every other st so the knit sts are on one needle held in front, and the purl sts are on the other needle held in back. Hold needles parallel and work the Kitchener Stitch to close the top cuff.

Finishing

Using C2 for the Kids, and C2 and C3 for the Adults, duplicate stitch a few random dots in the DOTS section.

Make second legwarmer to match.

Weave in ends, wash and block lightly.

Chevron Chart

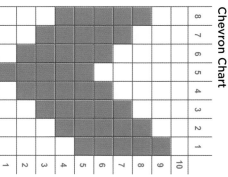

For child size, work Chevron Chart from bottom to top and from right to left every row. Work in C1 then in C2, then work Dots Chart. (For adult size, work in C1, then C2, then C3, then work Dots Chart.)

Dots Chart

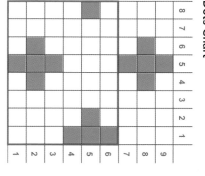

Work Dots Chart from bottom to top and from right to left for every row. For child size, work repeat section 2 times (for adult size, work it 3 times).

Legend

	knit knit stitch
	MC
	C1
	CC
—	pattern repeat

MERRIFIELD HAT

by Angela Baldi

FINISHED MEASUREMENTS

12 (14.75, 16, 17.25, 18.75, 20, 21.25)" circumference x 5.5 (6.25, 7.25, 9, 10, 11, 12)" high; hat is meant to be worn with 2" of negative ease.

YARN

Knit Picks Swish Worsted Brights (100% Superwash Merino Wool; 110 yards/50g): MC Pucker 26639, 1 ball.

Knit Picks Swish Worsted (100% Superwash Merino Wool; 110 yards/50g): C1 White 24662, C2 Wonderland Heather 26067, 1 ball each.

NEEDLES

US 8 (5mm) 16" circular needles, or size to obtain gauge.

US 8 (5mm) DPNs or two 24" circular needles for two circulars technique, or one 32" or longer circular needle for Magic Loop technique, or size to obtain gauge. You will need these for the tops of the hats, and you may find it easier to knit the newborn hat on these needles.

US 5 (3.75mm) DPN's, or 16" circular needles for larger sizes, or 3 sizes smaller than needle to obtain gauge.

NOTIONS

Yarn Needle

6 Stitch Markers, 1 of different color

Pom Pom Maker

GAUGE

18 sts and 24 rows = 4" over St st in the round, blocked.

Merrifield Hat

Notes:

This hat is inspired by playing in the snow and is designed for everyone in the family. The hat plays with texture and color to keep the knitting interesting. The three smallest sizes fit like a traditional beanie; the four largest sizes are designed to be slouchy. The pom pom is optional.

The two "tweed" stitch patterns call for slipping stitches with the yarn either in front or in back. As you're working, double check that you're holding the yarn in the correct position.

When the pattern calls for a new color, simply drop the previous color and begin working with the new. When you need to work with an already used color, carry it up the inside of the hat, unless you haven't worked with that color in over 4 rows. In that case, cut your yarn, leaving a 6" tail, and begin working with the color again in the new place. Weave in any loose ends when you're finished with the hat.

1x1 Rib (in the round over an even number of sts)

All Rounds: *K1, P1; rep from * to end of rnd.

Semi-Woven Tweed

Rnd 1: with C1, *Sl1 WYIB, K1; rep from * to end of rnd.

Rnd 2: with C1, K all sts.

Rnd 3: with MC, *Sl1 WYIF, K1; rep from * to end of rnd.

Rnd 4: with MC, K all sts.

Rnd 5: with C1, *K1, Sl1 WYIB; rep from * to end of rnd.

Rnd 6: with C1, K all sts.

Rnd 7: with MC, *K1, Sl1 WYIF; rep from * to end of rnd.

Rnd 8: with MC, K all sts.

Three Color Tweed

Rnd 1: with C2, *Sl1 WYIF, K1; rep from * to end of rnd.

Rnd 2: with C2, K all sts.

Rnd 3: with C1, *Sl1 WYIB, K1; rep from * to end of rnd.

Rnd 4: with C1, K all sts.

Rnd 5: with MC, *Sl1 WYIF, K1; rep from * to end of rnd.

Rnd 6: with MC, K all sts.

Rnd 7: with C2, *Sl1 WYIB, K1; rep from * to end of rnd.

Rnd 8: with C2, K all sts.

Rnd 9: with C1, *Sl1 WYIF, K1; rep from * to end of rnd.

Rnd 10: with C1, K all sts.

Rnd 11: with MC, *Sl1 WYIB, K1; rep from * to end of rnd.

Rnd 12: with MC, K all sts.

DIRECTIONS

Brim

Using your smaller needle and MC, loosely CO 54 (66, 72, 78, 84, 90, 96) sts. Join in the rnd, being careful not to twist your sts, and PM to indicate the start of the round. Work in 1x1 Rib for 1 (1, 1.5, 2, 2.25, 2.5)".

Body of Hat

Switch to your larger needle, K 2 (2, 2, 2, 2, 4, 4) rnds.

Semi-Woven Tweed

Work Rnds 1-4 of Semi-Woven Tweed 1 (1, 1, 1, 1, 1, 1) time.

Work Rnds 5-8 of Semi-Woven Tweed 0 (0, 0, 1, 1, 1, 1) time.

Three Color Tweed

Work Rnds 1-6 of Three Color Tweed 1 (1, 1, 1, 1, 1, 1) time.

Work Rnds 7-12 of Three Color Tweed 0 (0, 0, 1, 1, 1, 1) time.

With C1, K 2 (2, 4, 4, 4, 4, 6) rnds.

Crown

From this point, you will be working with only C2.

K 1 (1, 3, 7, 9, 11, 12) rnds. On the last rnd, PM after every 9 (11, 12, 13, 14, 15, 16) sts. You now have 6 stitch markers, including the marker for the start of the rnd.

You will now begin decreasing the top of the hat. When you need to, switch to your needles for small diameter circular knitting.

Sizes 12 (14.75, 16)" ONLY:

Rnd 1: *K to 2 sts before M, K2tog; rep from * to end of rnd. 6 sts dec.

Rnd 2: K all sts.

Repeat Rnds 1 and 2 a total of 5 (7, 8) times, until 24 sts remain.

Next Rnd: *K2, K2tog; rep from * to end of rnd. 18 sts.

Next Rnd: *K1, K2tog; rep from * to end of rnd. 12 sts.

Next Rnd: *K2tog; rep from * to end of rnd. 6 sts.

Sizes 17.25 (18.5, 20, 21.25)" ONLY:

Decrease Rnd: *K to 2 sts before M, K2tog; rep from * to end of rnd. 6 sts dec.

Repeat the Decrease Rnd a total of 11 (12, 13, 14) times, until 12 sts remain.

Next Rnd: *K2tog; rep from * to end of rnd. 6 sts.

All Sizes

Break your yarn and draw through the remaining live sts, closing the top of the hat.

Finishing

Weave in ends, wash and block.

Pom Pom

Make a pom pom that is 2 (2, 2, 3, 3, 3, 3)". Use either one color or alternate the three yarn colors so that the pom pom is a blend of all three. Sew the pom pom securely to the top of the hat.

GARMOND SOCKS

by Emily Ringelman

FINISHED MEASUREMENTS

Women's S (M, L, XL): 7 (8, 9, 10)" finished leg and foot circumference, unstretched; choose a size 1-2" smaller than your actual foot circumference. 7" leg length.

YARN

Knit Picks Stroll (75% Superwash Merino Wool, 25% Nylon; 231 yards/50g): MC Dove Heather 25023, C1 White 26082, C2 Tranquil 26083; 1 ball each

NEEDLES

US 1.5 (2.5mm) DPNs or two 24" circular needles for two circulars technique, or one 32" or longer circular needle for Magic Loop technique, or size to obtain gauge

NOTIONS

Yarn Needle
Stitch Marker

Gauge

32 sts and 48 rows = 4" in St st in the round, blocked.

Garmond Socks

Notes:

These socks are worked from the cuff down with contrast color cuffs, heel flaps, and toes. The leg and foot are worked in three-round stripes in two different colors. These socks are a great use for those leftover bits of sock yarn!

Mistake Rib Stitch Pattern (worked in the round over a multiple of 4)
Round 1: *K2, P2; rep from * to end.
Round 2: K1, *P2, K2; rep from * to last 3 sts, P2, K1.
Rep Rnds 1-2 for pattern.

Kitchener Stitch (grafting)
With an equal number of sts on two needles, break yarn leaving a long tail and thread through yarn needle. Hold needles parallel, with WS's facing in and both needles pointing to the right. Perform Step 2 on the first front st, and then Step 4 on the first back st, and then continue with instructions below.
1: Pull yarn needle K-wise through front st and drop st from knitting needle.
2: Pull yarn needle P-wise through next front st, leave st on knitting needle.
3: Pull yarn needle P-wise through first back st and drop st from knitting needle.
4: Pull yarn needle K-wise through next back st, leave st on knitting needle.
Repeat Steps 1-4 until all sts have been grafted.

DIRECTIONS

Cuff
With C2, CO 56 (64, 72, 80) sts and divide over needles. PM and join to work in the round, being careful not to twist sts.

Work in Mistake Rib Stitch for 2". Break C2.

Leg
Rounds 1-3: With MC, K.
Rounds 4-6: With C1, K.

Do not break yarn between stripes; twist the two yarns together on the inside at each color change, and carry the unused yarn loosely up the inside.

Continue to work in three-round stripes until leg measures 7", or to desired length to top of heel flap, ending with a complete three-round stripe. Do not break yarn.

Heel
Switch to C2. Heel flap is worked back and forth in rows over half of the total sts.

Heel Flap Row 1 (RS): *Sl 1, K1; rep from * 14 (16, 18, 20) times. Turn work.
Heel Flap Row 2 (WS): Sl 1, P27 (31, 35, 39).
Repeat the last two rows 15 times more; 16 slipped sts per side.

Next Row (RS): K17 (19, 21, 23), SSK, K1, turn.
Next Row (WS): Sl 1, P6, P2tog, P1, turn.
Next Row: Sl 1, K to 1 st before gap, SSK to close gap, K1, turn.

Next Row: Sl 1, P to 1 st before gap, P2tog to close gap, P1, turn.
Repeat the last two rows until all heel sts have been worked.
Break C2.

Gusset and Foot
Return to top of heel flap where you left the stripe yarn. Using the next color in the sequence, PU 16 sts down side of heel flap, K across heel sts, PU 16 sts along heel flap, K across foot sts. This is the new beginning of rnd.

Gusset Decrease Round: K1, SSK, K to 3 sts before end of second heel flap, K2tog, K1, K across foot sts. 2 sts dec.
Next Round: Knit.

Continuing to work in three-round stripes, repeat the last two rounds until 56 (64, 72, 80) sts remain.

Work in three-round stripes until foot measures 1.75" shorter than desired length, ending after a full three-round stripe is complete. Total sock length should be about 1 (1.25, 1.5, 1.5)" shorter than actual foot length for a proper fit.

Toe
Switch to C2. Break MC and C1.

Round 1: *K1, SSK, K22 (26, 30, 34), K2tog, K1; rep from twice. 52 (60, 68, 76) sts.
Round 2: Knit.
Round 3: *K1, SSK, K to 1 st before decrease, K2tog, K1; rep from twice. 4 sts dec.
Round 4: Knit.

Repeat Rounds 3-4 a total of 2 (2, 3, 4) times, 44 (52, 56, 60) sts; then repeat only Round 3 7 (8, 9, 9) times. 16 (20, 20, 24) sts remain.

Divide remaining sts into top and bottom sts, 8 (10, 10, 12) on each of two needles.

Use a yarn needle and the Kitchener stitch to join toes.

Finishing
Weave in ends, wash and block to Finished Measurements.

CHIRONAX COWL

by Joyce Fassbender

FINISHED MEASUREMENTS

21" circumference x 6.5" (back) & 16.5" (front) depth

YARN

Knit Picks Capretta (80% Merino, 10% Cashmere, 10% Nylon; 230 yards/50g): Cream 25600, 2 balls

NEEDLES

US size 5 (3.75mm) 16" circular, or size to obtain gauge

NOTIONS

Yarn Needle
Stitch Markers
Cable Needle

GAUGE

22 sts and 28 rows = 4" over pattern, blocked.

For pattern support, contact joycef2@gmail.com

Chironax Cowl

Notes:

Charts A and B are worked flat. Odd rows are worked from right to left. Even rows are worked from left to right. Charts C, D, and E are worked in the round. Odd and even rows are worked from right to left.

Boxed areas of charts indicate the stitch pattern repeat across rows.

Use stitch markers between pattern repeats if necessary. Stitch markers between stitch pattern repeats will need to be repositioned while working charts and between charts.

K2tog Bind Off

K2, slip sts onto left needle, K2tog TBL. *K1, slip sts onto left needle, K2tog TBL.* repeat * until all sts are bound off.

DIRECTIONS

Set Up Rows

Cast on 5 sts using long tail cast on.

Row 1 (RS): K1, M1, K3, M1, K1. 7 sts.
Row 2 (WS): K1, M1, P5, M1, K1. 9 sts.

Work Charts

Work odd and even rows of charts A and B as: K2, work chart, K1, work chart again, K2.

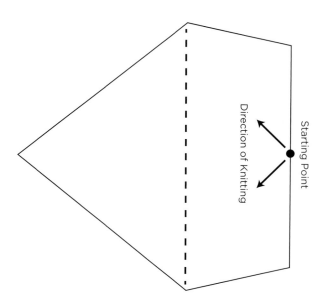

Direction of Knitting

Starting Point

Work Chart A one time. 45 sts.
Work Chart B four times. 173 sts.

Join in the round, taking care not to twist. Continue working charts C, D, and E in the round.

Work Chart C one time. 189 sts.

Odd rows of Chart C: Work Chart C1, K1, work Chart C2.
Even rows of Chart C: Work Chart C1, P1, work Chart C2.

Work Chart D one time. 201 sts.

Odd rows of Chart D: Work Chart D1, K1, work Chart D2.
Even rows of Chart D: Work Chart D1, P1, work Chart D2.

Work Chart E one time. 217 sts.

Odd rows of Chart E: Work Chart E1, K1, work Chart E2.
Even rows of Chart E: Work Chart E1, P1, work Chart E2.

Finishing

Bind off loosely using the K2tog Bind Off. Weave in ends. In order to obtain the correct shape, the cowl will need to be blocked. To block, soak in warm water for 20 minutes, remove excess water, then block aggressively. Fold in half along the front and back edges. Pin the following order: 1) pin the top straight, 2) pin the front edge straight, 3) pull out and pin the bottom edge points, and 4) pin the back edge.

Chart A

Legend

No Stitch
Placeholder - No stitch made.

make one right
Place a firm backward loop over the right needle, so that the yarn end goes towards the back

knit
RS: knit stitch
WS: purl stitch

make one left
Place a firm backward loop over the right needle, so that the yarn end goes towards the front

ssk
Slip one stitch as if to knit, slip another stitch as if to knit. Insert left-hand needle into front of these 2 stitches and knit them together

yo
yarn over

k2tog
Knit two stitches together as one stitch

purl
RS: purl stitch
WS: knit stitch

2/1 LPC
RS: sl2 to CN, hold in front. p1, k2 from CN
WS: sl1 to front. p2, k1 from CN

quadruple yo
RS: yo four times
WS: k 1st yo, p 2nd yo, k 3rd yo, p 4th yo

pattern repeat

cable 4 front
sl 2 to CN, hold in front. k2, k2 from CN

cable 4 back purl
sl2 to CN, hold in back. k2, p2 from CN

cable 4 front purl
sl 2 to CN, hold in front. p2, k2 from CN

cable 2 back purl
sl1 to CN, hold in back. k1, p1 from CN

cable 2 back
sl1 to CN, hold in back. k1, k1 from CN

cable 2 front
sl1 to CN, hold in front. k1, k1 from CN

cable 4 back
sl2 to CN, hold in back. k2, k2 from CN

cable 2 front purl
sl1 to CN, hold in front. p1. k1 from CN

2/1 RPC
RS: sl1 to CN, hold in back. k2, p1 from CN
WS: sl2 to back. k1, p2 from CN

p2tog
Purl 2 stitches together

p2tog tbl
Purl two stitches together in back loops, inserting needle from the left, behind and into the backs of the 2nd & 1st stitches in that order

Chart B

Chart C1

Chart C2

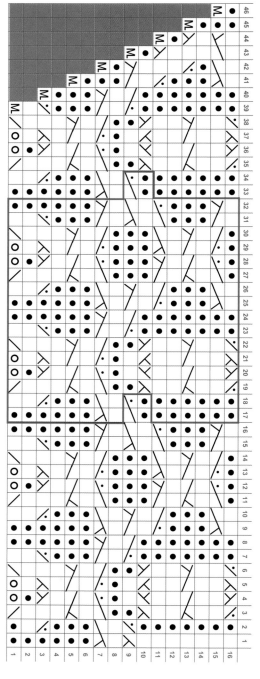

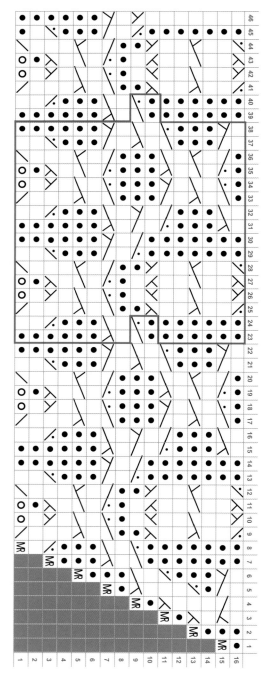

Chart D1

Chart D2

MOSSBANK HEADBAND

by Erica Jackofsky

FINISHED MEASUREMENTS

4 (4)" width x 18 (20.5)" length/
circumference

YARN

Knit Picks The Big Cozy (55% Superfine
Alpaca, 45% Peruvian Highland Wool; 44
yards/100g): Finnley Heather 26488, 1 ball

NEEDLES

US 13 (9mm) straight or circular needles, or
size to obtain gauge

NOTIONS

Yarn Needle

Cable needle

GAUGE

10 sts and 12 rows = 4" in St st, blocked.

14 sts & 15 rows = 4" in pattern, blocked

For pattern support, contact Erica@FiddleKnits.com

Mossbank Headband

Notes:

Don't like gauge swatches? Use the first 15 rows of the pattern to check your gauge. If you reach 4" then you're working at the recommended tension.

The larger size is 8 rows (approximately 2") longer than the small. Both sizes are worked the same through row 22.

For the cast on you have two choices. Use a provisional cast on and then graft the ends of the headband together at the end or cast on as normal and sew the ends together.

C2x1 left purl – Cable 2 over 1 Left Purl
Slip 2 to cable needle and hold in front. Purl 1, Knit 2 from cable needle.

C2x1 right purl – Cable 2 over 1 Right Purl
Slip 1 to cable needle and hold in back. Knit 2. Purl 1 from cable needle.

C2x2 left – Cable 2 over 2 Left
Slip 2 to cable needle and hold in front. Knit 1, Knit 2 from cable needle.

C2x2 left purl – Cable 2 over 2 Left Purl
Slip 2 to cable needle and hold in front. Purl 2. Knit 2 from cable needle.

C2x2 right – Cable 2 over 2 Right
RS: slip 2 sts to cable needle and hold in back. Knit 2. Knit 2 from cable needle.

C2x2 right purl – Cable 2 over 2 Right Purl
Slip 2 to cable needle and hold in back. Knit 2. Purl 2 from cable needle.

DIRECTIONS

Size Small
Cast on 6 sts.

Row 1: Slip 1, K5
Row 2: Slip 1 WYIF, K1, P2, K1, P1
Row 3: Slip 1, K5
Row 4: Slip 1 WYIF, K1, P2, K1, P1
Row 5: Slip 1, K1, YO, K2, YO, K2
Row 6: Slip 1 WYIF, K1, P2tbl, P2, P1tbl, K1, P1
Row 7: Slip 1, K1, YO, K4, YO, K2
Row 8: Slip 1 WYIF, K1, Kltbl, P4, Kltbl, K1, P1
Row 9: Slip 1, K1, P1, YO, K4, YO, P1, K2
Row 10: Slip 1 WYIF, K2, Kltbl, P4, Kltbl, K2, P1
Row 11: Slip 1, K1, P2, YO, c2x2 left, YO, P2, K2
Row 12: Slip 1 WYIF, K3, Kltbl, P4, Kltbl, K3, P1
Row 13: Slip 1, K1, P2, c2x2 right Purl, c2x2 left Purl, P1, K2
Row 14: Slip 1, K1, P2, K4, P2, K2, P1
Row 15: Slip 1, c2x1 right Purl, P4, c2x1 left Purl, K2
Row 16: Slip 1 WYIF, K1, P2, K6, P2, K1, P1
Row 17: Slip 1, K1, c2x1 left Purl, P4, c2x1 right Purl, K2
Row 18: Slip 1 WYIF, K1, P2, K4, P2, K2, P1
Row 19: Slip 1, K1, P1, c2x2 left, c2x2 right, P1, K2
Row 20: Slip 1 WYIF, K2, P8, K2, P1

Size Large
Cast on 6 sts.

Row 1: Slip 1, K5
Row 2: Slip 1 WYIF, K1, P2, K1, P1
Row 3: Slip 1, K5
Row 4: Slip 1 WYIF, K1, P2, K1, P1
Row 5: Slip 1, K1, YO, K2, YO, K2
Row 6: Slip 1 WYIF, K1, P2tbl, P2, P1tbl, K1, P1
Row 7: Slip 1, K1, YO, K4, YO, K2
Row 8: Slip 1 WYIF, K1, Kltbl, P4, Kltbl, K1, P1
Row 9: Slip 1, K1, P1, YO, K4, YO, P1, K2
Row 10: Slip 1 WYIF, K2, Kltbl, P4, Kltbl, K2, P1
Row 11: Slip 1, K1, P2, YO, c2x2 left, YO, P2, K2
Row 12: Slip 1 WYIF, K3, Kltbl, P4, Kltbl, K3, P1
Row 13: Slip 1, K1, P2, c2x2 right Purl, c2x2 left Purl, P1, K2
Row 14: Slip 1 WYIF, K1, P2, K4, P2, K1, P1
Row 15: Slip 1, K1, YO, K2, YO, K2
Row 16: Slip 1 WYIF, K1, YO, K2, YO, K2
Row 17: Slip 1, K1, P2tbl, P2, P1tbl, K1, P1
Row 18: Slip 1 WYIF, K2, P4, K1, K1, ssK, P1
Row 19: Slip 1, K1, P2, K2, P4, K2, ssK, P1
Row 20: Slip 1 WYIF, K1, P2, c2x2 left, P2, K2
Row 21: Slip 1, K1, P1, K8, P1, K2
Row 22: Slip 1 WYIF, K2, P8, K2, P1
Row 23: Slip 1, K1, P1, c2x2 left, c2x2 right, P1, K2
Row 24: Slip 1 WYIF, K2, P8, K2, P1
Row 25: Slip 1, K1, P1, K8, P1, K2
Row 26: Slip 1 WYIF, K2, P8, K2, P1
Row 27: Slip 1, K1, P1, c2x2 right, c2x2 left, P1, K2
Row 28: Slip 1 WYIF, K2, P8, K2, P1
Row 29: Slip 1, K1, P1, K8, P1, K2
Row 30: Slip 1 WYIF, K2, P8, K2, P1
Row 31: Slip 1, K1, P1, c2x2 right Purl, c2x2 left Purl, P1, K2
Row 32: Slip 1 WYIF, K2, P2, K4, P2, K2, P1
Row 33: Slip 1, K1, P2, c2x1 right Purl, P4, c2x1 left Purl, K2
Row 34: Slip 1 WYIF, K1, P2, K6, P2, K1, P1
Row 35: Slip 1, c2x1 left Purl, P4, c2x1 right Purl, K2
Row 36: Slip 1 WYIF, K2, P2, K4, P2, K2, P1
Row 37: Slip 1, K1, P1, c2x2 left, c2x2 right, P1, K2
Row 38: Slip 1 WYIF, K2, P8, K2, P1
Row 39: Slip 1, K1, P1, K8, P1, K2
Row 40: Slip 1 WYIF, K2, P8, K2, P1
Row 41: Slip 1, K1, P1, c2x2 left, c2x2 right, P1, K2
Row 42: Slip 1 WYIF, K2, P8, K2, P1
Row 43: Slip 1, K1, P1, K8, P1, K2
Row 44: Slip 1 WYIF, K2, P8, K2, P1
Row 45: Slip 1, K1, P1, c2x2 right, c2x2 left, P1, K2
Row 46: Slip 1 WYIF, K2, P8, K2, P1
Row 47: Slip 1, K1, P1, K8, P1, K2
Row 48: Slip 1 WYIF, K2, P8, K2, P1
Row 49: Slip 1, K1, P1, c2x2 right Purl, c2x2 left Purl, P1, K2
Row 50: Slip 1 WYIF, K2, P2, K4, P2, K2, P1
Row 51: Slip 1, K1, c2x1 right Purl, P4, c2x1 left Purl, K2
Row 52: Slip 1 WYIF, K1, P2, K6, P2, K1, P1
Row 53: Slip 1, K1, c2x1 left Purl, P4, c2x1 right Purl, K2
Row 54: Slip 1 WYIF, K2, P2, K4, P2, K2, P1
Row 55: Slip 1, K1, P1, c2x2 left Purl, c2x2 right Purl, P1, K2
Row 56: Slip 1 WYIF, K2tog, K2, P4, K2, ssK, P1
Row 57: Slip 1, K1, P2, c2x2 left, P2, K2
Row 58: Slip 1 WYIF, K2tog, K1, P4, K1, ssK, P1
Row 59: Slip 1, K1, P1, K4, P1, K2
Row 60: Slip 1 WYIF, K2tog, P4, ssK, P1
Row 61: Slip 1, K7
Row 62: Slip 1 WYIF, K1, P2tog tbl, P2tog, K1, P1
Row 63: Slip 1, K5
Row 64: Slip 1 WYIF, K1, P2, K1, P1

Row 68: Slip 1 WYIF, K2tog, P4, ssK, P1
Row 69: Slip 1, K7
Row 70: Slip 1 WYIF, K1, P2tog tbl, P2tog, K1, P1
Row 71: Slip 1, K5
Row 72: Slip 1 WYIF, K1, P2, K1, P1

Finishing

Weave in ends and block lightly. Sew, or graft, the cast on and last row together.

Row 11: Slip 1, K1, P2, YO, c2x2 left, YO, P2, K2
Row 12: Slip 1 WYIF, K3, K1tbl, P4, K1tbl, K3, P1
Row 13: Slip 1, K1, P1, c2x2 right Purl, c2x2 left Purl, P1, K2
Row 14: Slip 1 WYIF, K2, P2, K4, P2, K2, P1
Row 15: Slip 1, K1, c2x1 right Purl, P4, c2x1 left Purl, K2
Row 16: Slip 1 WYIF, K1, P2, K6, P2, K1, P1
Row 17: Slip 1, K1, c2x1 left Purl, P4, c2x1 right Purl, K2
Row 18: Slip 1 WYIF, K2, P2, K4, P2, K2, P1
Row 19: Slip 1, K1, P1, c2x2 left, c2x2 right, P1, K2
Row 20: Slip 1 WYIF, K2, P8, K2, P1
Row 21: Slip 1, K1, P1, K8, P1, K2
Row 22: Slip 1 WYIF, K2, P8, K2, P1
Row 23: Slip 1, K1, P1, c2x2 left, c2x2 right, P1, K2
Row 24: Slip 1 WYIF, K2, P8, K2, P1
Row 25: Slip 1, K1, P1, K8, P1, K2
Row 26: Slip 1 WYIF, K2, P8, K2, P1
Row 27: Slip 1, K1, P1, c2x2 right, c2x2 left, P1, K2
Row 28: Slip 1 WYIF, K2, P8, K2, P1
Row 29: Slip 1, K1, P1, K8, P1, K2
Row 30: Slip 1 WYIF, K2, P8, K2, P1
Row 31: Slip 1, K1, P1, K8, P1, K2
Row 32: Slip 1 WYIF, K2, P8, K2, P1
Row 33: Slip 1, K1, P1, c2x2 right Purl, c2x2 left Purl, P1, K2
Row 34: Slip 1 WYIF, K2, P2, K4, P2, K2, P1
Row 35: Slip 1, K1, c2x1 right Purl, P4, c2x1 left Purl, K2
Row 36: Slip 1 WYIF, K1, P2, K6, P2, K1, P1
Row 37: Slip 1, K1, c2x1 left Purl, P4, c2x1 right Purl, K2
Row 38: Slip 1 WYIF, K2, P2, K4, P2, K2, P1
Row 39: Slip 1, K1, P1, c2x2 left, c2x2 right, P1, K2
Row 40: Slip 1 WYIF, K2, P8, K2, P1
Row 41: Slip 1, K1, P1, K8, P1, K2
Row 42: Slip 1 WYIF, K2, P8, K2, P1
Row 43: Slip 1, K1, P1, K8, P1, K2
Row 44: Slip 1 WYIF, K2, P8, K2, P1
Row 45: Slip 1, K1, P1, c2x2 left, c2x2 right, P1, K2
Row 46: Slip 1 WYIF, K2, P8, K2, P1
Row 47: Slip 1, K1, P1, K8, P1, K2
Row 48: Slip 1 WYIF, K2, P8, K2, P1
Row 49: Slip 1, K1, P1, c2x2 right, c2x2 left, P1, K2
Row 50: Slip 1 WYIF, K2, P8, K2, P1
Row 51: Slip 1, K1, P1, K8, P1, K2
Row 52: Slip 1 WYIF, K2, P8, K2, P1
Row 53: Slip 1, K1, P1, K8, P1, K2
Row 54: Slip 1 WYIF, K2, P8, K2, P1
Row 55: Slip 1, K1, P1, c2x2 right Purl, c2x2 left Purl, P1, K2
Row 56: Slip 1 WYIF, K2, P2, K4, P2, K2, P1
Row 57: Slip 1, K1, c2x1 right Purl, P4, c2x1 left Purl, K2
Row 58: Slip 1 WYIF, K1, P2, K6, P2, K1, P1
Row 59: Slip 1, K1, c2x1 left Purl, P4, c2x1 right Purl, K2
Row 60: Slip 1 WYIF, K2, P2, K4, P2, K2, P1
Row 61: Slip 1, K1, P1, c2x2 left Purl, c2x2 right Purl, P1, K2
Row 62: Slip 1 WYIF, K2tog, K2, P4, K2, ssK, P1
Row 63: Slip 1, K1, P2, c2x2 left, P2, K2
Row 64: Slip 1 WYIF, K2tog, K2, P4, K2, ssK, P1
Row 65: Slip 1, K1, P2, c2x2 left, P2, K2
Row 66: Slip 1 WYIF, K2tog, K1, P4, K1, ssK, P1
Row 67: Slip 1, K1, P1, K4, P1, K2

Size Small Chart

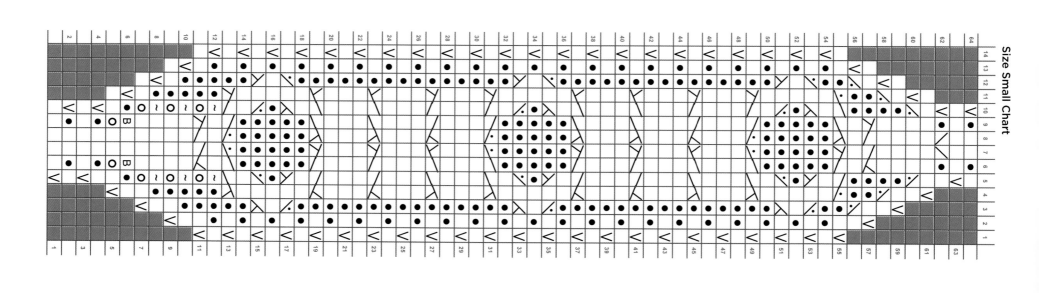

Size Large Chart

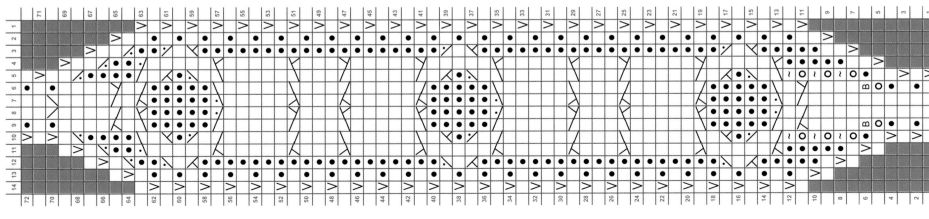

Legend

no stitch
placeholder - no stitch made.

slip
RS: Slip stitch as if to purl, holding yarn in back
WS: Slip stitch as if to purl, holding yarn in front

knit
RS: knit stitch
WS: purl stitch

purl
RS: purl stitch
WS: knit stitch

yo
yarn over

knit tbl
RS: Knit stitch through back loop
WS: Purl stitch through back loop

purl tbl
RS: Purl stitch through the back loop
WS: Knit stitch through the back loop

c2 over 2 left
sl2 to CN, hold in front. k2, k2 from CN

c2 over 2 right P
sl2 to CN, hold in back. k2, p2 from CN

c2 over 2 left P
sl 2 to CN, hold in front. p2, k2 from CN

c2 over 1 right P
sl1 to CN, hold in back. k2, p1 from CN

c2 over 1 left P
sl2 to CN, hold in front. p1, k2 from CN

c2 over 2 right
sl2 to CN, hold in back. k2, k2 from CN

p2tog tbl
RS: Purl two stitches together in back loops, inserting needle from the left, behind and into the backs of the 2nd & 1st stitches in that order
WS: Slip one stitch as if to knit, Slip another stitch as if to knit. Insert left-hand needle into front of these 2 stitches and knit them together

p2tog
RS: Purl 2 stitches together
WS: Knit 2 stitches together

k2tog
RS: Knit two stitches together as one stitch
WS: Purl 2 stitches together

ssk
RS: Slip one stitch as if to knit, Slip another stitch as if to knit. Insert left-hand needle into front of these 2 stitches and knit them together
WS: Purl two stitches together in back loops, inserting needle from the left, behind and into the backs of the 2nd & 1st stitches in that order

Abbreviations

BO	bind off	M	marker		stitch	TBL	through back loop
cn	cable needle	M1	make one stitch	RH	right hand	TFL	through front loop
CC	contrast color	M1L	make one left-leaning	rnd(s)	round(s)	tog	together
CDD	Centered double dec		stitch	RS	right side	W&T	wrap & turn (see
CO	cast on	M1R	make one right-lean-	Sk	skip		specific instructions
cont	continue		ing stitch	Sk2p	sl 1, k2tog, pass		in pattern)
dec	decrease(es)	MC	main color		slipped stitch over	WE	work even
DPN(s)	double pointed	P	purl		k2tog: 2 sts dec	WS	wrong side
	needle(s)	P2tog	purl 2 sts together	SKP	sl, k, psso: 1 st dec	WYIB	with yarn in back
EOR	every other row	PM	place marker	SL	slip	WYIF	with yarn in front
inc	increase	PFB	purl into the front and	SM	slip marker	YO	yarn over
K	knit		back of stitch	SSK	sl, sl, k these 2 sts tog		
K2tog	knit two sts together	PSSO	pass slipped stitch	SSP	sl, sl, p these 2 sts tog		
KFB	knit into the front and		over		tbl		
	back of stitch	PU	pick up	SSSK	sl, sl, sl, k these 3 sts		
K-wise	knitwise	P-wise	purlwise		tog		
LH	left hand	rep	repeat	St st	stockinette stitch		
		Rev St st	reverse stockinette	sts	stitch(es)		

Palette
Fingering Weight
100% Peruvian Highland Wool

Wool of the Andes
Worsted Weight
100% Peruvian Highland Wool

Wool of the Andes
Fingering Weight
100% Peruvian Highland Wool

Stroll
Fingering Weight
75% Superwash Merino Wool,
25% Nylon

Wool of the Andes Superwash
Worsted Weight
100% Superwash Wool

Wool of the Andes Sport
Sport Weight
100% Peruvian Highland Wool

Gloss Fingering
Fingering Weight
70% Merino Wool, 30% Silk

Galileo
Sport Weight
50% Merino Wool, 50% Viscose
from Bamboo

Swish DK
DK Weight
100% Superwash Merino Wool

Big Cozy
Super Bulky Weight
55% Superfine Alpaca,
45% Peruvian Highland Wool

Gloss DK
DK Weight
70% Merino Wool, 30% Silk

Lindy Chain
Fingering Weight
70% Linen, 30% Pima Cotton

Capretta
Fingering Weight
80% Merino Wool, 10% Cashmere,
10% Nylon

Brava Bulky
Bulky Weight
100% Premium Acrylic

Swish Worsted
Worsted Weight
100% Superwash Merino Wool

View these beautiful yarns and more at www.KnitPicks.com